RUDOLF STEINER (1861–1925) called his spiritual philosophy 'anthroposophy', meaning 'wisdom of the human being'. As a highly developed seer, he based his work on direct knowledge and perception of spiritual dimensions. He initiated a modern and universal 'science of spirit', accessible to anyone willing to exercise clear and unprejudiced thinking.

From his spiritual investigations Steiner provided suggestions for the renewal of many activities, including education (both general and special), agriculture, medicine, economics, architecture, science, philosophy, religion and the arts. Today there are thousands of schools, clinics, farms and other organizations involved in practical work based on his principles. His many published works feature his research into the spiritual nature of the human being, the evolution of the world and humanity, and methods of personal development. Steiner wrote some 30 books and delivered over 6000 lectures across Europe. In 1924 he founded the General Anthroposophical Society, which today has branches throughout the world.

STRENGTHENING THE WILL

The 'Review Exercises'

RUDOLF STEINER

Selected and compiled by Martina Maria Sam

RUDOLF STEINER PRESS

Translated by Matthew Barton

Rudolf Steiner Press
Hillside House, The Square
Forest Row, RH18 5ES

www.rudolfsteinerpress.com

Published by Rudolf Steiner Press 2010

Originally published in German under the title *Rückschau, Übungen zur Willensstärkung* by Rudolf Steiner Verlag, Dornach, in 2007. This authorized translation is published by permission of the Rudolf Steiner Nachlassverwaltung, Dornach

A catalogue record for this book is available from the British Library

ISBN: 978 1 85584 238 0

Cover by Andrew Morgan Design
Typeset by DP Photosetting, Neath, West Glamorgan
Printed and bound in Malta by Gutenberg Press

Mixed Sources
Product group from well-managed forests, and other controlled sources
www.fsc.org Cert no. TT-CoC-002424
FSC © 1996 Forest Stewardship Council

The paper used for this book is FSC-certified and totally chlorine-free. FSC (the Forest Stewardship Council) is an international network to promote responsible management of the world's forests.

Contents

Note to the Reader

Given that this volume is largely made up of quotations from Rudolf Steiner's works, in order to keep a consistent flow to the language, tone and terminology we judged it best to translate afresh Rudolf Steiner's words from the latest and most accurate German editions. To aid English readers in finding English editions of the relevant works, a list of published translations is given on page 103.

('GA' stands for *Gesamtausgabe* or Collected Works of Rudolf Steiner in the original German.)

About this Book

The importance of Rudolf Steiner's review exercises for the path of anthroposophical schooling cannot be valued too highly. Review and meditation can be seen as the two pillars of self-development which, with the supplementary or accompanying exercises spanning them like an arch, form the gateway through which we can enter into conscious experience of the spiritual realm.

Meditation leads thinking back to its living source by thoroughly warming it. The supplementary exercises educate our life of feeling by establishing a healthy balance between inner and outer, sympathy and antipathy, while the review exercises cultivate the will by penetrating it with powers of consciousness.

Whereas meditation enlivens thinking by intentionally creating an interior space in which a thought or image can unfold, review brings the sleeping experience of our daily lives to awareness. By directing our attentive gaze to what has happened—whether in a single day or in whole phases of life—we kindle light in our will life. Heeding Rudolf Steiner's suggestion that we undertake this review backwards, in reverse sequence, or also look on what has happened from a kind of 'external perspective', requires a huge inner effort as we distance ourselves from daily experiences.

The very strong effects of the review exercises, which Steiner highlights, can be explained by the 'jolt' to the psyche from freeing oneself from events in this way. As the following compilation shows, over a period of about 20 years Steiner gave a surprising range of suggestions for carrying out such exercises, whose specific qualities can also develop other corresponding capacities.

The first form of the exercise is the *review of the day* (Chapter 1) as an end to each day for those pursuing a path of spiritual schooling. This sort of review was originally laid down as follows as a requirement for every member of the 'Esoteric School of Theosophy': 'Before going to bed, the pupil must look back on the day and evaluate his own conduct.'[1] But the very diverse ways in which this can be done become apparent through Rudolf Steiner's different, specific suggestions. What is common to all the exercises of this type is that the review of the day should be conducted in reverse sequence—a requirement not yet contained in the rules of the 'Esoteric School'. In this way, a pupil not only makes his daily life into a continual schooling but also gradually acquires a new sort of 'imaginative memory' to replace what one might call 'mechanical memory'. This prepares him for modes of perception in the world of spirit. The review exercise enables us to pursue ideas beyond the threshold of conscious awareness and grasp them in their original vitality.

To complement this, Rudolf Steiner recommends that from time to time we undertake *life review exercises* (Chapter 2). In other words, we can conjure up our own past deeds and experiences as though another person had done or experienced them. In this type of review, we have to encounter ourselves as we would another. By this means our higher being is awoken within our daily self, and we can become aware of the 'overlighting I being in the ordinary ego'.[2]

This life review exercise can be enhanced by focusing during meditative contemplation on the *impact of others* in our own biography, vividly imagining 'what each person by our side has done for us' (Chapter 3). By this means we develop the capacity, when we encounter another person, to receive a picture of his 'true being'.

A specific variant of the review exercise can also be found in the so-called *greater karmic insight exercise* (Chapter 4), which can develop our insight into karmic connections and the spiritual workings of destiny.

A key aspect of review exercises which Rudolf Steiner increasingly accentuated over the years—whether through the daily review or through imagining plays or tunes in reverse sequence—is that of a general *cultivation of the will* (Chapter 5). When we detach our conceptual powers from the external course of events, the will can free itself from its body-bound state. By doing so it gains strength and becomes more 'transparent', thereby itself becoming an organ of spiritual perception. In this way the pupil achieves the stage of intuitive knowledge at which he lives his way into the world of spirit, as a being among spiritual beings. The pupil can support this type of will exercise by others such as ridding himself of particular habits.

The review exercise enables us not only to prepare ourselves for participation in the world of spirit but also for *life after death* (Chapter 6). The daily review integrates into our awareness what the soul experiences every night. Whether we know it or not, at night our soul gazes back on the events of the day in reverse sequence, at the same time passing moral judgement on our own experiences. This nightly experience in turn forms the basis for kamaloka after death: the period during which, after laying aside the etheric body, we work through the life that has just passed. The review exercises during our lifetime can, as it were, enable us to accomplish some of this after-death work in advance.

The few suggestions Steiner made for will exercises in education, and getting children to imagine things in reverse, offer further insights (Chapter 7). However, his astonished and almost annoyed reply to a question shows clearly that children should never be asked to practise the review exercise as part of some kind of spiritual schooling.

I have not included here anything relating to the so-called 'will' or 'initiative' exercise that forms part of the supplementary exercises. The companion volume on these six exercises contains all passages relevant to this.

The seven chapters of this book are an attempt to compile and thematically arrange Steiner's numerous suggestions for practising review or reverse-sequence exercises. The passages in each section are arranged chronologically (although excerpts from written works are placed first because of their greater authenticity as compared with lecture transcripts). What became clear in this process, surprisingly, was that the sequence of chapters also gives rise to something approaching chronological order.

Thus, over the years of Rudolf Steiner's activity, the review exercises acquire a kind of spiritual time-body.

Chapter 1, on the review of the day, contains written stimulus for Rudolf Steiner's pupils and instructions drawn from the early period of his esoteric work. Gradually, alongside this, general life review exercises arose with the aim of awakening the pupil's higher being. At the time of the First World War, with its attendant social catastrophes, Rudolf Steiner modified the review exercises to awaken the social capacities we so sorely need today. This involves acquiring true imaginations of the other that can form in us during human encounter. The karma exercises which Steiner suggested at a later date have a similar effect, and can lead to a conscious grasp of karmic connections. In public lectures in the 1920s, Steiner went on to emphasize the two pillars of inner schooling: the enlivening of thinking through meditation and the cultivation and illumination of will life by means of the review exercises. These now find their place as key exercises for will development, and Steiner repeatedly emphasizes how greatly they aid the pupil in grasping essential qualities of the world of spirit.

It is of course not true to say that each new aspect of this progression overrides the validity of a previous one. Instead, the outstanding importance of these review exercises is accentuated by the diversity of Steiner's suggestions, from which each of us can choose what speaks individually to us.

When reading this compilation we should not of course forget that the majority of excerpts are drawn from the larger and often complex context of whole lectures, which were presented to a specific group of people in response to a particular situation. For further study the reader is referred to relevant volumes in the complete edition of Steiner's works. However, in collected works as rich and extensive as Steiner's, a comparison between his comments on particular themes invariably gives rise to surprising new perspectives and insights. One can say that the dynamic qualities of a living spiritual configuration only become discernible when observed and illumined from a range of different angles, through the fact that individual aspects mutually illumine, shape and support one another. This applies equally to the will exercises on the path of inner schooling, with the 'review' exercise at their core.

Martina Maria Sam

1. Review of the day—transforming the power of memory

Each day one should review one's daily experiences. You can do this by picturing to yourself the most important things you experienced during the day and the way you behaved in relation to them. All this is done in a frame of mind that wishes to *learn* from life. How can I improve on something I did today? This is the kind of question one asks oneself, and it does not dull one's sense of either joy or suffering. On the contrary, you will become more sensitive. But you will not harbour anxiety and regret about what you did, instead transforming such feelings into the intention to do things better in future. Thus you work on yourself like a builder. Just as a builder does not sit down disconsolately in front of a house he has built, complaining sadly about it, but instead, when he comes to build again, uses the experiences he has gained to do it better, so a person can do the same in regard to himself. Sorrow and regret can drag us down whereas learning builds us up. Sorrow and regret are of no use. The time we waste in entertaining these feelings should be used instead for our own improvement. All this requires no more than three or four minutes and then you will fall asleep with a manas[3] that has received the capacity to progress. If one can add to this an important precept for life or also a good thought for others, this is especially good. This gradually as it were transforms us, since we have endowed the manas liberated

in sleep from all personal limitations with a worthy content that nurtures our development.
(Early April 1904)[4]

[...] Then you can take four or five minutes to undertake a review of your experiences during the day. I would ask you to let these daily experiences pass briefly before your soul and to be clear how you relate to them. Observe yourself and ask to what extent you are satisfied, how you could have experienced things differently, what you could have done better. Thus you become your own observer. The point of this is to observe yourself from a higher perspective so that gradually the 'higher self' comes to hold sway over your everyday self. At the same time, all worry, sorrow or suchlike about what you experienced should fall away. We should simply learn from our own lives, read them like a book. We should not think back regretfully to the past—we can do that the rest of the day if necessary—but courageously use this past for the future. Then we will learn something that benefits our current, personal existence, and that will, above all, bear fruit in the period after our death.
(2 August 1904)[5]

In the evening before falling asleep, one should briefly review what one experienced during the day. There is no need for this to be comprehensive but it is important, instead, that one evaluates and judges oneself as if one was someone else. One should learn from oneself. Life should increasingly become a lesson. One starts with the evening and works backwards to the morning.
(End of 1904)[6]

In the evening before falling asleep each pupil should cast his gaze back to how he lived during the day. This is not about allowing the maximum number of events to pass before your soul but about doing this with the most important events. We can ask ourselves what we can learn from what we experienced or did that day. In this way life becomes a lesson for us. Our stance towards ourselves is that of learning from each day to benefit every new day. By doing this we take our past with us into the future and prepare our immortality. Then perhaps we can end the day by thinking of other, beloved people who might need our good thoughts.

If you fall asleep during this exercise it really doesn't matter. If you do, then you take a tendency to progressive development with you into sleep—and that's good too. Only the morning meditation must take place from beginning to end in an alert and wakeful state. I would just ask you to accomplish the evening review backwards, in other words starting with events that just happened, in the evening, and working your way back to the morning.
(2 January 1905)[7]

If you intervene in your own life of soul in this way and regulate it, you will also develop the ability to observe yourself so that you regard your own affairs with the kind of composure with which you would regard someone else's. To be able to look at one's own experiences, one's own joys and sufferings, as though they were someone else's is a good preparation for spiritual schooling. You will gradually achieve what is necessary here by daily reviewing the images of what you experienced. In doing so you should perceive yourself pictorially within your experiences; in other words, observe yourself in your daily life as though from without. You can gain a certain practical capacity for such self-observation if you start by imagining specific, small details of this daily life. You can increasingly develop your ability to conduct this kind of review so that after much practice you will find you can accomplish it fully in only a short space of time. This reverse review of experiences is especially important for spiritual schooling because it allows the soul to free itself from its otherwise inherent tendency to trace in thought *only* the course of sensory events. By thinking in reverse you picture events accurately but not bound by their normal, sensory trajectory; and this is something you need for penetrating the supersensible world. This strengthens the imaginative capacity in a healthy way. This is why it is good not only to picture your daily life but also other things in reverse sequence—for instance the plot of a play, a story, or a melody, etc. Increasingly the spiritual pupil will develop the ideal of relating to events that approach him in life with inner certainty and composure, not judging them according to his own frame of mind but according to their own inner significance and value. By nurturing this ideal he will create the fundamental stance of soul that enables him to devote himself to the contemplation of symbolic and other ideas and thoughts, as described earlier.

(Occult Science, 1910)[8]

In the evening, not too long before you go to bed:

Undertake a brief review of the events of the day, lasting four or five minutes. This should be done in reverse sequence: in other words, first picture what you did in the evening then the experiences you had as you work back towards the morning. Then you can focus on one of the remembered events of the day and picture it vividly, as if it were an object before your eyes. This picturing capacity will become more developed as you keep practising, so that it gradually becomes like a picture, an imagination. Then you should focus your awareness entirely on the following words:

> What I experienced today
> stands spiritually before me now;
> so place yourself my I
> spiritually before the picture:
> feel how you felt
> before it in the day;
> be alone with it.[9]

Then try to pass over into meditative contemplation with the following words, sensing and feeling everything it is possible to experience through them:

> I wish to learn
> in the I of the spirit:
> to be as in body
> to feel as in body
> to love as in body.
> I wish to live in the light,
> I wish to perceive in the light.[10]

Try to focus your awareness on what one can feel through these words, excluding all other thoughts. Then try to free your awareness entirely from these thoughts too, and allow

entry to no others. If you reach the stage of being able to do this, ideas will come to you from the world of spirit: either in imaginative form (as forms and figures) or as inspirations (without figure or form).
(18 April 1912)[11]

In the evening, not too long before you go to bed:

Undertake a short review of the day lasting four or five minutes. This should run backwards so that you first picture what you experienced in the evening and then work your way back to the morning's experiences. After this, try to picture an experience you had years ago which you can remember clearly enough for it to stand vividly before the soul, with the certainty of fact. Once you have pictured this image in a full and vivid way, try to imagine how you would relate to this experience now, trying to imaginatively conjure the picture of what would arise from this experience if you could reawaken it and deal with it as you are now. You should then try to imaginatively grasp what arises from the experience in this way, and then (in meditation) immerse yourself in the following thoughts:

In a similar way I will one day (probably only in a future incarnation) confront such an event and will then have to conduct myself as I was unable to before, but now am able to.

You can engage in this way with the same experience for many weeks on end; and then take another such experience, again for many weeks. Through this meditation a time will eventually arrive when the knowledge surfaces from the soul,

as though in a picture, that karmic residues remain from all one's experiences, and that these must be realized in future lives. While you form these thoughts you must however exclude all other thoughts from your awareness. Then you will become aware of the spiritual working of karma.
(18 April 1912)[12]

Then [after meditating], a specific event from the evening is evoked as image and imagined backwards. One should feel oneself to be standing outside it. Then take a similar such event from earlier in the day, and a third from still earlier, until you arrive back at the morning. The events will then join up by themselves so that you acquire a tableau of the day in a relatively short time. Any idea of regret should be kept away, but instead you should form an idea of how you might behave better in future if something similar occurs. Immediately before falling asleep you should try to imbue yourself with the thought: 'Into me enter from the spirit what I most need.'
(undated)[13]

Everything we call memory is connected with the astral body.[14] The idea you formed yesterday is still there in you but it has no chance to remain there if it is not embedded in the astral body—if it does not stimulate resonances that persist, and today once again recall your experience from yesterday. Now it is not possible for someone to make any progress at all in developing his astral body without working to enhance his capacity for memory.

I have spoken of how we need to work at a strict control of thinking, at mastering the whole of our thought life, of how we need to be clear that our thoughts are real processes—and that it is profoundly untruthful to say that 'thoughts are duty-free' and that no one can observe our thoughts. Anyone who wishes to develop a real capacity for vision has to work on his power of memory. We can only do so by preventing our memories from simply rising above the horizon of consciousness in chaotic fashion then sinking down again below it.

How do our memories actually pass through our awareness? They come and go and we give ourselves over to them. We are driven by memories that surface and sink again. As long as this is the case, we are also given up to all incidents and influences which are continually exerted upon the astral body from without. This can only be overcome by devoting ourselves each day, if only for a short period, to cultivating our memory. This must of course not prevent us from fulfilling all our daily obligations. That is the first rule of theosophy—that no one should be deterred from his ordinary profession by pursuing a spiritual path. In fact, just a few minutes spent each day on cultivating memory can do wonders for our astral body.

What we need to achieve can be described in a few words: we need to make our life an opportunity to school ourselves, to learn. Life is a school for only a very few people. Most people give themselves up to joy and pain. And the life they experience passes them by, in a sense, with its pain, joy and contentment, for they learn nothing from it. The theosophist says, in contrast: 'Each new day must be a stage in my development.'

This is why the theosophist allows no day to pass without

reviewing in spirit, with the eye of spirit, the important events of his day. The best moment for this is the last moment we pass in a waking state—in other words, the moment immediately before falling asleep. If we are able to spend two, three, four or five minutes filling ourselves with the day's experiences, allowing them to pass before us in an objective sense, then we will do much to enhance the astral body.

During the day we feel joy and pain, pleasure and contentment. The theosophist has no need to dull his senses or his experience of life but he should, rather, experience vivid sympathy and antipathy during the whole of his ordinary daily life. No one should be able to distinguish him from others in this respect. He should only distinguish himself from others during those four, five to twenty minutes when, instead of allowing feelings of joy and pain, pleasure and contentment to pass through him in the usual way he reflects instead on what they have taught him: What did joy and pain bring me? What did contentment and discontent show me? Was this joy or pain justified? Couldn't I have had a different view of them? Couldn't I have responded differently to comfort or discomfort? Couldn't I have some influence on the course of events? Did I act as I would always wish to act? Did I act in a way that I can see as being in harmony with the whole harmony of the universe? In other words, one raises one's daily life to a higher standpoint.

If we observe our feelings during these four, five to twenty minutes, and re-experience them—not so that we merely recreate the same impression but observe them objectively so that we see our seeing, hear our hearing and get clarity about our pain and joy, become clear whether our joy and pain were perhaps due to our own triviality, and thus discover our whole stance in the world—then we learn something from our experiences and are working to develop our astral organs.

Those who develop clairvoyance on the astral plane can see how a person's astral body changes if he is alert and attends to such exercises for many years. His astral body will start to be inwardly organized. Whereas it was once chaotic, a real hotchpotch—you can see grotesquely winding snakelike lines in human astral bodies—now certain forms arise in it, regular forms, and it starts to become differentiated.

People usually cannot see these things today, but cultivating the memory is the means that enables us to see this transformation both in ourselves and in our fellow human beings. What happens to us today becomes our experience tomorrow; and experience is the measure against which we can evaluate what happens to us in future. This enhances our development and organizes our astral body. However insignificant it may appear, it has a reliable effect. It helps open our spiritual eyes so that they can see into the feelings of others and can really become capable of perceiving the world of spirit.

(21 February 1904)[15]

Review: When we practise the review it is good to transpose ourselves into what we experienced in such a way that we fully sense the difference between our soul experience and the actual experience in the external world; this is like the difference between observing the image of a landscape with closed eyes, that is, in memory, and observing it with eyes open—direct perception in other words. It is the same relationship as that between memory and review. (Memory is recall whereas, in this case, review is like direct perception.)

In an initiate, memory gradually vanishes and is replaced by direct perception of what one wishes to recall. One needs to invoke a precise picture of one's daily experiences with every detail clearly evoked—shirt, face, manner, etc., all very precise—and observe what happened in the image: *how* one spoke, *what* was done, etc. etc. It is very much to do with recalling little things that do not seem so interesting, things one finds hard to remember, for this stimulates one's inner powers. The power of imagination is formed by the capacity to create such pictures. There is no need to recall absolutely everything but just to form very clear pictures. No muscle must be exerted while undertaking all this work.
(20 January 1907) [16]

Proper practice of the review awakens a great power in the soul; and we need this to rise eventually to the astral plane.
(20 January 1907) [17]

Every evening before you go to sleep, review the events of the day in reverse sequence. The day should pass before us in images. An important aspect of this is that we ought never to let a sense of remorse arise. Remorse is always egotistic. Someone who regrets or is remorseful wishes he had been better, an entirely egotistic wish. We should not wish we had been better but should instead desire to become better. We should learn from our daily life. If we have done something badly, we should not regret it but think: at the time I was unable to act differently, but now I can and will do it better in future. In relation to every experience of the day we should ask ourselves: Did I do it right, couldn't I have done it better? One will always find that one could have done it better. Another thing is very important here also: to learn to observe ourselves as if we were someone else; as if we see and criticize ourselves from outside. Overall we should form as clear a picture of the day as possible. It is much more important to be able to remember small details than important circumstances. A military commander who was involved in a fierce battle will have the picture of the battle in his mind in the evening. It will engrave itself into his soul by itself. But all the small details of the day—for instance how he put on and took off his boots—have faded from his mind. And this is what is important: to form as complete a picture of the day as possible. For example, we can observe ourselves crossing the road and try to recall how the rows of houses looked, which shop windows we passed, who we encountered on the way and what they looked like; and what we ourselves looked like. Then we might see ourselves entering a shop and recall who the shopkeeper or sales attendant was who came to serve us—what she was wearing, how she spoke and moved, etc. To recall such little details we have to exert ourselves considerably, and this strengthens the powers of the soul.

Don't imagine that this will take a whole hour. Initially you will recall only a few things, and then gradually, with increasing effort, more and more. By practising you will eventually be able to let the whole day with all its details pass before your soul in five minutes like a series of tableaux. But patience is needed to achieve this. This exercise will be of no use at all to you if you go over the day's events quickly and mechanically, merely registering them in a colourless kind of way.

The aim of this exercise is as follows. If someone goes for a long walk and at the end of his journey wishes to gain a sense of the path he has travelled, he can do this in one of two ways. Firstly, he can keep his back turned to the path and try to recall what lies behind him. Or he can turn round and gain an overview of the path he has taken. Now when we have completed a journey through time we can only initially recall it in memory rather than actually *looking* back over what we experienced. Yet this looking back, as we know it only in spatial terms, is also possible in the temporal realm, and we can learn this by trying to let the past day pass again before us in a clear, vivid, pictorial way. No past event has passed entirely: it is all still there, inscribed in what we call the Akashic record. Only by this means can we learn to read it. Initially, by doing so, we only perceive there what relates to ourselves; but gradually other things come into view too. This is why the evening review is such an important and indispensable exercise.

The esoteric pupil can discover something remarkable about himself: he will gradually notice that his memory gets worse and worse. This is a quite natural development. But soon it will get better again or, to put it more precisely, his memory will fade and something new will replace it. This new element is the capacity to see the past directly and immediately. Then one no longer needs ordinary memory.

(29 January 1907)[18]

The evening review is also important. It must be done in reverse since we should accustom ourselves to the mode of perception of the astral plane. During the review everything should be pictured as vividly as possible. To begin with, of course, you can't vividly evoke all eighty or so important experiences of the day—you have to choose among them carefully, until eventually the whole of your daily life can unfold before you like a tableau. Here again it is much more a matter of little, apparently insignificant actions, for the effort needed to recall these is precisely what awakens the powers of the soul.

(6 June 1907)[19]

And finally the review. Don't look back on 'important' things but, on the contrary, on unimportant ones; and do so from the end back to the beginning. Memory is the bridge which leads us to the invisible chronicle. Streets, fields, flowers, stones and so forth are available for us to look back on either by recalling them in memory or by really looking back on them with our eyes. This occurs in the original temporal sequence. But there is another way to look back or review things: as if the temporal sequences were unfolding in space. Our so-called memory is lost but something higher is gained. The direction is reversed because everything flows from the end towards the beginning in the higher worlds, and so the pupil must be prepared for this. The review should be accomplished without remorse, for this is egotistic.

(20 and 27 June 1907)[20]

As he falls asleep the esoteric pupil should say to himself, 'I am returning to my creators', and on awakening, 'I come

from where I existed before my body was created.' And in meditation he should remain conscious for a few moments in these realms. If he does this with this stance of soul, he will kindle in himself the sacred fire, the inner warmth that he needs. And before he falls asleep in the evening, he should develop these same feelings during his evening esoteric work, even if only in the form of the daily review. By allowing pictures of his day to pass before him in reverse sequence, he creates spiritual images which he takes with him as essence into worlds of spirit. This must be done backwards because that is how everything happens in the spiritual worlds. Thus one finds access to these worlds so that they flow into us more easily and we into them. In normal 'forwards' thinking which we bear with us into worlds of spirit we in fact oppose their flow, push them away from us and therefore obstruct our development and ourselves.
(15 April 1909)[21]

It can also often happen that a meditating person thinks that he has fallen asleep while doing the review; but when he awakens and tries again to trace what has occurred in him in the meantime, he will often find that the review has in fact continued in him. It is very important to feel this. It does not contradict what has always been said about not according importance to what occurs without the I's participation. By recalling what has occurred in our memory, we in fact incorporate it into the I.
(8 November 1912)[22]

If we assume that someone has fallen asleep while doing his review, nevertheless he will wake up again. If he then recalls

the point he had reached in this exercise, then he will realize that his meditation continued in sleep although his waking consciousness was extinguished. In certain circumstances this can be of more use to him than a meditation conducted in full awareness, for it is a significant fact that his consciousness continued to work in the disembodied state, and that a transition occurred from normal waking consciousness to a higher state of consciousness. This is already an expansion of awareness, and it represents real progress.
(6 January 1913)[23]

At the moment a pictured thought sinks down into the unconscious and is preserved there until memory re-evokes it, a supersensible process occurs, a really supersensible process. In fact, if you can trace this process, consisting of the sinking of a conscious thought into the unconscious and remaining there as image—if, in other words, you pursue a pictured thought to its locus in the unconscious—then you are already slipping into the supersensible realm. Just consider that if you accomplish the usual process of memory, the pictured thought must first resurface into consciousness, and you then preserve it here, up above in consciousness, never below in the unconscious. You have to make a clear distinction between normal memory and the pursuing of thoughts down into the unconscious. What occurs in memory can be compared with a swimmer who sinks below the surface of the water and whom you can still see until he is completely submerged. Now he is below and you can no longer see him. When he resurfaces you see him again! The same thing happens with human thoughts: you have them as long as they remain on the physical plane; if they dive under, you forget them. When you remember them they surface again like the swimmer. But this process I'm referring to, which already tends towards imaginative insight, could be likened instead to you immersing yourself too, so that the swimmer doesn't fade from your gaze but you can still see him below you in the water.

But we can conclude from this nothing other than that the line I drew before to represent the surface—below which the thought sinks into the unconscious, into the capacity for memory—is the threshold to the world of spirit itself, its first threshold. This follows with absolute necessity. It is the first threshold to the world of spirit! Just consider how close people stand to this threshold of the world of spirit.

And now think of a process whereby one might try to get down there, really to dive below the surface. The process would involve making efforts to trace the path of thoughts down into the unconscious. This can actually only happen by trying. It can be done by trying the following thing for example. Assume you have formed a thought in relation to the external world; now try to invoke the memory process artificially, independently of the outer world. I recommend a way to do this in *Knowledge of the Higher Worlds*: in the very standard rules for reviewing the events of the day. If you gaze back on the day's events you practise finding a way into the paths which the thought itself takes when it submerges and resurfaces. In other words, the whole process of remembering is intended to pursue the thoughts which have sunk down beneath the threshold of consciousness.

But the same passage in *Knowledge of the Higher Worlds* also states that it is a good idea to trace the thoughts you have formed in reverse sequence, that is from their end back to the beginning, and, if you are reviewing the day, to trace the sequence of events backwards from the evening to the morning. In doing this you have to make a different kind of exertion from the one required in normal remembering. It is this exertion that as it were gets you beneath the threshold of consciousness, enabling you to grasp the picture you had of the experience. And as you try to do this you will begin to sense and inwardly experience how you are following the thoughts, pursuing them down beneath the threshold of consciousness. This really is a process of inner, experiential testing. But you have to undertake this review in a serious frame of mind—not losing your impetus or regard for the seriousness of the undertaking. Keep trying to accomplish this review process for a longer period, or indeed the process of fetching an experience up out of the memory, fetching up an experienced world of thought by picturing it in reverse— thus exerting yourself more than you have to in the normal sequence of recall—and you will also find that at a certain point you are no longer able to take hold of the thought in the way you used to do in ordinary life on the physical plane.

On the physical plane memory takes a form—and it is best for memory on the physical plane if it does this—in which the thought one wishes or tries to recall surfaces in accordance with its original context, in a way corresponding to how the original thought was formed on the physical plane. But by gradually accustoming oneself to pursuing the thoughts below the threshold of consciousness, one finds them down there in a form different to how they appear in ordinary life.

This is the mistake that people always make when they think they will find in the world of spirit a mere copy of what exists in the physical world. You have to assume that thoughts below the threshold will look different. In reality, below the threshold of consciousness they appear as if all that characterizes them on the physical plane has been stripped away. There below they appear entirely as pictures, and certainly ones in which we sense life. We feel them to be full of life. It is very important to attend to this phrase: we feel life in them. Only when you have a sense that a thought is starting to live and breathe can you be quite sure that you have really pursued it below the threshold of consciousness. I explained the same thing from a different point of view when I compared rising to imaginative perception with placing your head in an anthill. I said then that everything starts to come to life, to wriggle and move about.

For example, let's assume that during the day—to take a very ordinary experience—you sat down at a table and picked up a book. Then, at some time in the evening you vividly imagine how it was: the table, the book, you yourself sitting there—as if you are outside yourself. And it is always a good idea to picture everything in pictorial form, not in abstract thoughts, for abstraction, the capacity to abstract, has no significance at all for the imaginative world. So you form this picture: sitting at a table with a book in your hand. All I mean with the table and book is that you should picture some scene from your daily life as vividly as possible. Then, if you really let your inner gaze rest upon this picture, if you imagine it in really intensive meditation, from a certain moment onwards you will feel different from before; yes, as a comparison, I'd say that this will feel rather like picking up a living creature.

[...]

This difference you feel between touching a dead or living thing is something you should be clear about. If you pick up a lifeless object you feel something different from when you touch a living creature. When you conceive a thought on the physical plane the sense you get is one that can be compared with picking up a lifeless thing. But the moment you really dip down beneath the threshold of consciousness, this changes, and you get a sense instead that the thought has inner life and starts to move about. You discover the same thing—to use a comparison for a feeling in the soul domain—as when, for instance, you pick up a mouse. The thought moves, tickles and prickles.

(18 September 1915)[24]

2. Review of events in your life—awakening the higher self

The esoteric pupil[25] must detach himself from his daily life for a brief while and occupy himself with things that are entirely different from his normal preoccupations. He should also attend to these other things in a way quite different from how he usually fills his day. This does not mean that what he accomplishes during these periods of reflection has nothing to do with the content of his daily work. On the contrary, you will soon find that setting aside such moments in the *right* way will give you all the strength you need to attend to your daily tasks. Nor should you think that observing these rules might leave you less time to perform your duties. *Five minutes each day will do if you really have no more time available.* How you spend these five minutes is what matters.

During this time you should wrest yourself free from daily life. Your thoughts and feelings should acquire a different quality and colouring from normal. Let your joys, sufferings, cares, experiences and deeds pass before you; and everything that you otherwise ordinarily experience should now be observed from a higher perspective. Think for a moment of how, ordinarily, we regard what someone else has experienced or done in a very different way from what we ourselves experience. This is inevitable, for we are deeply involved in what we ourselves do or feel, while we only observe the deed or experience of another. In these moments of detached reflection we must try instead to look upon our own experiences and deeds, and evaluate them as if someone else had done or experienced them. Think for a moment of someone who has suffered a sad misfortune. He will have a quite different sense of this than if the same thing happens to someone else. No one can say this is wrong, for it is human nature. That's an extreme example, but the same applies in every daily circumstance. The esoteric pupil must set aside certain moments when he seeks the capacity to confront himself as he would another. He must look from without upon himself with the inner composure of someone who makes an objective assessment. If you can do this, your own experiences will appear to you in a new light. As long as you are intertwined with them, you are involved as much with the inessential as the essential. If you acquire the inner composure of the overview, then the essential detaches from the inessential. Distress and joy, every thought and decision, appear different when you observe yourself in this way. It is rather like spending a whole day in a village and seeing everything from close up, both big and small things; then, in the evening, climbing a nearby hill and looking down again on the whole place. Suddenly the different parts of the village appear in a quite different relationship from what you see when you're down there in the midst of it. This does not have to work for strokes of destiny you're currently experiencing; but the spiritual pupil must try to accomplish it with things that have happened some time ago. The value of such inner, calm self-reflection is much less to do with *what* you observe in the process than with finding the *strength* in yourself that develops this inner composure.

Besides what we might call our 'daily self' we all bear

within us a higher nature as well. This higher nature remains concealed until awoken. And you can only awaken it yourself. While this higher self goes on slumbering, the higher capacities that lead to supersensible perceptions likewise remain hidden and slumbering.
(GA 10, 1904)[26]

If you reflect on yourself you will soon see that apart from the self-encompassing thoughts, feelings and conscious will impulses, you also bear within you a second, more powerful self. You can become aware that you are subject to this second self as to a higher power. Initially, it is true, you will experience this second self as a lower kind of nature compared with your clear, fully conscious psyche, which tends to seek for what is good and true. And you may try to overcome this lower nature. But if you examine yourself more closely, this second self can in fact teach you something different. If you regularly review what you have done or experienced you will make a remarkable discovery, one that assumes ever greater importance as you grow older. If you ask yourself what you did or said during this or that period of your life, you will find that you did all kinds of things that you really only come to understand at a later date: things you did seven or eight or even twenty years ago, which you clearly see you can only understand now, a long time later. Many people never discover this because they do not attend to it. But it is extraordinarily useful for us to regularly commune with ourselves. At the point where you become aware that in earlier years you did things you only now begin to understand—for your insight was not yet mature enough then to

understand what you did or said—the following feeling arises in your soul: you feel safe, protected by a good power which holds sway in your own depths; you begin to find ever-increasing trust in the fact that really, in the highest sense, we are not alone in the world and that everything we can understand and become aware of is truly only a small part of what we accomplish in the world.
(GA 15, 1911)[27]

One can learn to perceive in oneself something that appears to the psyche as a second, inner being. This becomes particularly apparent if we connect it with thoughts that show us how we bring about a set of destined circumstances in ordinary life. After all, we can see that a particular circumstance would not have arisen if we hadn't behaved in a certain way in the past. What happens to someone today arises in many instances from what he did yesterday. With the aim of developing our soul experience and insight further we can review our previous experience, seeking everything that shows how we ourselves laid the ground for subsequent destined occurrences. We can try to go back in time in this review to the point when a child awakens to consciousness: to the point when his memory begins. If we undertake a review of our life with a mood of soul that excludes our ordinary selfish sympathies and antipathies in response to strokes of destiny, we will see when we reach back in memory to the point in childhood I referred to, that it was then that the possibility first arose for us to feel things inwardly and to work consciously on our life of soul. This 'I' of ours was also there before this however; it worked in us, not with our conscious knowledge but nevertheless it developed in us the capacity which made us capable of knowing, capable of everything else we are aware of. This kind of stance towards our own destiny in life can give rise to something that no logical train of thought allows. We learn to look on strokes of destiny with composure; we see them approach us without prejudice; and yet we also see ourselves in the being who brings these events towards us. And when we look at life like this, our soul perceives the determining factors in our own destiny, already present at our birth, as connected with our own self. We wrestle our way through to the insight that the way we have worked upon ourselves since we came to consciousness is also how we worked before this consciousness awoke. By working our way through to a higher I being within our ordinary ego we not only find it possible to think of this higher I being in theoretical or conceptual terms but also to sense the living being of this 'I' in its reality as inner power in us, and to experience our ordinary ego as a creation of this other and higher I. To feel this represents a real beginning of vision of the soul's spirit being. And if it leads to nothing this is merely due to the fact that one does not carry it beyond this beginning. Such a beginning can be a scarcely noticeable, dull kind of feeling and may remain so for a long time. Yet if you strongly and conscientiously pursue what led to this beginning, you will ultimately come to a vision of the soul as spirit being.

(GA 16, 1912)[28]

A good way, open to all, of acquiring greater clarity about oneself consists in setting aside moments in one's life, at least once a year—perhaps on one's birthday. Then we should ask ourselves: what good and bad deeds have I done during this last period? If we scrutinize ourselves seriously we will find in most cases that our good deeds do not derive from our own personality but that we let them arise from an inner impetus. This inner impulse is our guardian angel who drives us to our good deeds. On the other hand we shouldn't just rely on this entirely and at every opportunity think merely that our guardian angel will inspire us—that would be misguided. If we did so, our guardian angel would soon leave us, in a certain respect at least.

If we continue to practise this exercise for a number of years, we will find that, more than anything else, drawing up these 'accounts' helps us to perceive and improve the flaws in our character. We will gradually prepare ourselves to pursue the esoteric path in a fruitful way by increasingly freeing ourselves from our own personality, and in a certain sense making ourselves empty so that the Christ principle can enter us—as Paul says: 'Not I, but Christ in me.'
(29 March 1911)[29]

We can have the following experience. Let's assume that someone in their youth who had not yet encountered anthroposophy read a novel and was unable to get it out of their mind; he would keep recounting and retelling it. Now later on, imagine that he reads another novel after embarking on an anthroposophical path. No sooner has he read it than he's forgotten it! He cannot recount what happens in it. But if there's a book that one either thinks is worth reflecting on or that someone else tells us is, we can undertake the following.

We read it through once, then immediately afterwards we try to go through it again in our mind—not just going over it but doing so backwards, from the end to the beginning, taking the last things first and the first last. Then, if we also take the trouble to go through certain details a second time, connecting strongly with it, and if we even take a piece of paper and write down short notes about it, and try to ask what aspect of this subject particularly interests us, then we will find that we develop a quite different kind of memory. This is no longer the same sort of memory. We can easily perceive the difference when we use it. When we invoke mechanical recall then things enter our soul as ordinary memories. But if, as esotericist or anthroposophist, one systematically develops the kind of memory I have referred to, then it seems as if the things we have experienced in this way stand still in time. We learn as it were to look back in time, and it really seems as if we are seeing the reality of what we observe there. We will find that things become increasingly pictorial, that our memory becomes ever more imaginative. Having done something of the kind I have described with a book, then, when you need to bring the matter to your attention again, you just have to engage with something connected with it and you will, as it were, find yourself looking back to the point of time when you were preoccupied with the book: you will see yourself reading it. This is not a memory: the whole picture rises up; and you will notice that whereas before you only read the book, now things actually rise up before you. You can see them as though at a temporal distance, and memory then becomes looking at pictures that stand at a distance in time. This is the very first beginning, the very basic primer for gradually learning to read the Akashic record: memory is replaced by learning to read in past time. And sometimes someone who has undergone a certain esoteric schooling may almost completely have lost his memory; but this will not harm him because he can see things unfolding in reverse sequence. He will see the things he himself was personally connected with in particular clarity. I'm telling you something that someone outside of anthroposophy would and can only mock if he heard it, for he will have no corresponding concept. If an esotericist says that he no longer has any memory and yet knows perfectly well what has happened because he gazes upon it in the past, the other will say: 'Sounds like an excellent memory to me!' This is because he can have no concept of the transformation that has occurred. In fact, this is based on a transformation in the etheric body.

As a rule this transformation of memory is also connected with something else too: with the fact that a kind of new evaluation of our inner nature arises. We cannot acquire this retrospective gaze without at the same time assuming a certain standpoint in relation to what we have experienced. Someone who at a later date looks back on something that he has engaged with in the way I described for studying a book—seeing himself in the midst of it—will inevitably judge whether attending to it was a clever or bad idea. This review is strongly connected with another experience, a kind of self-appraisal. One cannot do other than adopt a stance in relation to one's past. In relation to one thing we may reproach ourselves, and in relation to another we may be pleased that it succeeded. In other words, we will be unable to do anything other than evaluate the past we see unfolding

as we look back. We thus become sharper in appraising and evaluating ourselves, our past life. We feel, as it were, the etheric body coming alive, like something living incorporated in us that embodies our worth. Indeed, the etheric body changes in a way that often gives rise in us to an urge to engage in this kind of self-review: to gaze upon this or that so as to learn, very naturally, to appraise our worth as a human being. Whereas mostly people live their lives without perceiving it, now perception of the etheric body arises in the retrospective vision of one's own life. One's own life will gradually give one cause for concern when one undergoes an esoteric schooling. This is something we have to embrace: esoteric life can make work for us, can make us look more closely at both our good characteristics and flaws, at our errors and imperfections.
(22 March 1913)[30]

For many people who endeavour to progress on a spiritual path it would be good, as an exercise, to do the following from time to time, to do it repeatedly—to say: 'I will look back over the last three or four weeks or, even better, months, and will let important things pass before me in which I was involved. Quite systematically I will ignore all the injustices that may have been inflicted on me. I will exclude all that I say so often to excuse myself for what happens, such as that the other is to blame. I will never consider that another is more to blame than myself.' If we think how easily people tend to make others responsible, rather than themselves, for what they don't much like, it is clear how much good would come from reviewing one's life in this way: excluding the thought of an injustice even when an injustice has actually occurred, and allowing no criticism that the other might be wrong. Try this exercise—and you will find that you gain a quite different inner relationship to the world of spirit. Such things alter much in one's actual state of mind, in the real mood of the human soul.

(31 August 1913)[31]

3. Review from the other's perspective— awakening social impulses

You are opaque to yourself in your life of soul because you have memories. You are opaque because you have the capacity for memory.

You see, what gives us proper awareness of the physical plane is at the same time the reason why our normal consciousness cannot look into the realm that must underlie memory. It does really underlie memory. However, we can gradually try to reconfigure memory somewhat. We just have to be careful as we do so. We can begin by trying to invoke what we remember with ever greater precision in meditation, until we have the sense that memory is not just something we grasp hold of but something that stays put. Someone who develops an intensive, vibrant spiritual life gradually gains the feeling that memory is not something that comes and goes, arises and fades, but rather that the content of memory stands still. Now working in this way inevitably leads to a conviction that what otherwise surfaces in memory is in fact something that exists in stasis, that it really remains available as Akashic record, that it does not disappear. What we otherwise perceive in memory stands there in the world, exists in reality. But this method alone will not take us any further, for recalling only our personal experiences—leading to the insight that the content of memory remains static—is too egotistic to lead us beyond this conviction. In fact, if you were to over-develop this particular capacity of looking upon the fixity of your own experiences, you would in fact erect a real barrier to your vision of the free and autonomous world of spirit. Your own life would stand there in a still more compact form, obstructing your view.

Instead one can use a different method which, if I can put it like this, renders transparent the inscriptions in the Akashic record in a really excellent way. And once we look through the fixity of memories we can gain a sure view of the world of spirit with which we were united between death and a new birth. But for this we must not only draw on what remains static as memory from our own life—for this grows ever denser and more compact and then you really can't see through it any more. It has to become transparent. And it will become transparent if we make ever greater efforts not so much to remember what we have experienced from our own perspective but increasingly what has approached us from without. Instead of recalling what we learned, we can remember the teacher, the way he spoke, the way he seemed, what he did with or for us. We can recall how the book was written from which we learned this or that. Above all we recall the things that worked upon us by approaching us from the external world.

Goethe's book *Poetry and Truth* offers a wonderful way in to this, an instruction manual you might say. There Goethe describes how he was formed by his time; how various forces work upon him. Goethe was able to do this—to look back on his life not from the perspective of his own experiences but from that of others and the formative events of his time—because he was able to gain such deep insights into the world of spirit. But at the same time this is also the way to come into closer touch with the period which unfolded between our last death and our latest birth.

You see I'm directing your attention today, from a different angle, to the same thing I have already pointed out: expanding your interests beyond the personal, directing your interests and attention to what we are not, but what formed us, and from which we arose. One can see it as an ideal to look at our times and the longer periods that preceded us, and to seek there all the powers which formed this fellow one has become.

To describe it like this makes it seem fairly straightforward, but in fact it isn't an easy task. Yet because it requires a marked degree of selflessness, it is also a task that leads to great success. In particular, this method awakens the powers in us to enter with our I into the same sphere which the dead share with the living. In the not too distant future, focusing less on oneself and instead more on the nature of one's time will become a key aspect of education. I mean, getting to know one's time in a specific way, not as you find it nowadays in history books: the way this time or period has evolved quite naturally from spiritual impulses.

(17 December 1917)[32]

An essential power that is trying to develop in this fifth post-Atlantean epoch[33] is this: no longer to pass each other by, like ghosts, without forming a picture of the other and only defining the other human being through our abstract concepts. Really this is what we still do: we pass each other by like ghosts. One of the ghosts forms an idea that the other is a nice fellow, while the other thinks the first is not such a nice

fellow. Thinking someone is a bad person or a good one—
these are just abstract concepts. In our interpersonal
relations we have nothing other than a bundle of abstract
concepts. This is what has largely arisen from the Old Tes-
tament rule of 'making no graven image'; if we were to go on
in this way it would lead to the worst kind of antisocial life.
What radiates from deep within us, and wishes to be realized,
is that when one person encounters another a picture should
emerge and flow out—a picture of that particular state of
equilibrium which every individual person brings to
expression. However, this requires the kind of enhanced
interest which I have often described to you as the foundation
of society: the enhanced interest that each of us should take
in the other. Today we do not yet have an intense interest in
the other—which is why we criticize and judge him, form
judgements based on sympathies and antipathies rather than
the objective picture which wells up to meet us from the other
person.

This capacity to receive something like a mystic stimulus
when we encounter another is one that is trying to unfold. It
will enter life as a particularly social impetus. On the one
hand the consciousness soul[34] is striving to develop its full,
antisocial scope in this fifth post-Atlantean age. On the other,
something else is striving to emerge from within us: the
capacity to form pictures of those with whom we live, whom
we encounter in life. Social impetus and impulses—these
things lie a good deal deeper than we usually realize when we
speak of social and antisocial forces.

Now the following question may surface in you: how do we
gradually develop the capacity that allows a picture of

someone to emerge in this way? We have to acquire this capacity in life. At birth we bring with us Yahweh capacities that are simply given and which develop in the foetus. A culture of the future will not give human beings such an easy time: they will have to develop during their lifetimes the faculties they need to embody. Education will have to acquire much more specific and tangible principles than the ones which today create such havoc in children's schooling. Above all, an urge must be implanted in human beings to look back regularly on their life—but in the right way. The memories we often form of our early experiences still usually have a very selfish character. If we look back more selflessly on what we experienced during our childhood, youth and so on, depending on the age we are now, there emerge as though from the grey dawn of spiritual depths various people who participated in our life in the most diverse ways. Look back on your life, less focused on yourself and what interests you in your valuable self, but with more consideration of the figures who came towards you, bringing you up and educating you, becoming friends with you, nurturing you—or perhaps also harming you, sometimes even *harming you in a very beneficial way*. You will gain some insights from what surfaces there from the grey dawn of spiritual depths, from what approaches you. You will see how little, basically, we have cause to ascribe to ourselves what we become. Often something important in us is connected with our encounter at a certain point with this or that person, who, perhaps without his knowledge—or also very much with his knowledge—draws our attention to something. A really selfless review of our life consists, comprehensively, of all kinds of things that do not require us to gaze selfishly at our own navel but to extend our view to the figures who approached us at some point in our lives. If we attend very lovingly to what has come towards us, we will often see that what we had an antipathy towards at a certain time no longer evokes our antipathy once enough time has passed, for we see the inner connection. It may have been very useful or beneficial to us to have had an antagonistic contact with a particular person. Sometimes we benefit more from the negative thing someone does to us than from being nurtured or supported. It would be very useful for people to regularly undertake this kind of selfless review of life; and to imbue their lives with the conviction springing from this self-reflection that really they have very little cause to be so preoccupied with themselves! How much richer my life will be if I let my gaze turn to this or that person who entered this life of mine . . .

We free ourselves from ourselves as it were when we practise this kind of non-self-focused review. Then we get away from the terrible scourge of our times to which so many succumb—that of self-obsession. And it is so endlessly necessary that we do free ourselves from brooding on ourselves. Anyone who takes up the kind of self-reflection I have described will find that he is far too uninteresting to brood too much on his own life. Infinite light spreads across our life when we see it illumined by what enters this life from the grey dawn of spirit depths.

And this becomes fruitful for us: by this means we acquire the imaginative powers to encounter the other today in a way that allows something in him to appear that we would otherwise only become aware of after years, when we look

back to the figures who played a part in our earlier lives. Thus
we acquire the faculty to perceive real pictures of those whom
we encounter.
(7 December 1918)[35]

People today can spend years with others and know them no
better than they knew them when they first met. It really is
necessary that we counter the antisocial element with a social
one in future, in something like a systematic way. There are
various inner, psychological means to do this, for instance by
trying to look back on our own life on a regular basis, looking
back on this present incarnation and trying to gain an overview of what has occurred in our life between ourselves and
others who have played a part in this life. If we are honest,
most of us today will say that when we look back on our life
we place ourselves at the centre of everything, and the part
that all others have played appears more peripheral. We ask
what we gained from this or that person—a question based
on feelings. In fact this is something we should combat. We
should try to let pictures surface in us of people who intervened in our life in some way—teachers, friends, others who
nurtured us; or also those who harmed us and to whom, in
some respects we may owe more than to those from whom
we benefited. We should allow these pictures to pass before
our soul, and very vividly imagine what each person by our
side has done for us. If we do this we will see that we
gradually learn to forget ourselves, finding that almost every
attribute we have could not exist if one or another person had
not intervened in our life to nurture or teach us, or in some
other way. And only then, when we look back on long-gone

years and people we may no longer know, whom we more easily perceive objectively, we will see how the soul substance of our life is permeated by all that influenced us. Our gaze is broadened to include a host of people who touched our life at some time. If we try to gain a sense of how much we owe to one or another person, and in this way to see ourselves in the mirror of those who shared our lives and affected them, then gradually—and we will experience this—a sense emerges of something else: by practising forming pictures of people connected with us in the past, a sense issues from our soul that we can also form a picture of those whom we encounter now, in the present, whom we meet face to face each day. And it is enormously important that an urge awakens in us not to respond to someone we meet merely through sympathy or antipathy, not just to love or hate something in the other, but to awaken in ourselves a picture of what the other is really like, a picture devoid of love or hate. You may not consider that what I am saying now is particularly important. It *is* particularly important. This capacity to conjure in oneself an immediate picture of the other, to allow the other as it were to resurrect in our psyche, is a quality that is more or less vanishing with every passing week in humanity's evolution. Gradually human beings are losing this capacity entirely. They are passing each other by without kindling in themselves the urge to awaken the other within them. Yet this has to be consciously cultivated, and should also be included in children's education: the capacity to develop our imaginative powers in response to other people.

We can indeed really first develop our powers of imaginative perception through others if, rather than giving ourselves up to the sensations so commonly sought, we do not draw back from quietly looking back on our past relationships with others. Then we will also become able to develop an imaginative approach to those whom we meet in the present. And by doing so we are countering with a social impetus the antisocial impetus that is inevitably, increasingly and unconsciously developing. That is one aspect.

The other is something that can be linked to this review of our relationships with others: that we try to become ever more objective about ourselves. Again, we must go back to earlier stages of our life. But now we can, as it were, tackle things head-on: for instance when we're, let's say thirty or forty, we reflect on what it was like when we were ten years old. I do it like this: first I picture myself in the midst of the situation, but as if I were a different ten-year-old boy or girl; I try to forget for a moment that this was me. I really try to objectivize myself. This self-objectivization, this letting go in the present of my past, this peeling of the I out of its experiences, is something we should particularly strive for today—for the modern age tends to connect the I more and more with its experiences. People today want to live out quite instinctively what their experiences dictate, and this is why it is so difficult to engage in the activity that spiritual science offers. Each time one has to exert oneself anew rather than relying on what is given or has been retained. The comfortable status quo is of no use at all to real spiritual science. Things are forgotten and one has to keep cultivating them: but that's good, that is what is needed—to keep exerting oneself. Someone who is very advanced in spiritual science will try every day afresh to consider the most basic things, whereas others are ashamed to do so. In spiritual science nothing should rely on remembering something but instead on grasping hold of the present anew in direct experience.

We can attain this capacity by objectivizing ourselves—by picturing this little lad or lass at an earlier age as if he or she were someone else, not ourselves; by increasingly trying to free ourselves from our experiences, so that, as a thirty-year-old, we don't have to just go on repeating the ten-year-old's impulses. Freeing ourselves from our past is not the same as denying it, but instead we regain it in a different way. And this is something of enormous importance.

So on the one hand we consciously cultivate a social impetus through finding imaginative pictures for human beings here and now. We do this by looking back to people connected with us in the past, and seeing ourselves as having been formed by these people. On the other hand, by objectivizing ourselves in the past, we gain the capacity to directly develop our self-imagination. This self-objectivization in past periods of our life benefits us if it does not work unconsciously in us. You see, if the ten-year-old lad or lass goes on working in you, then you are really the thirty- or forty-year-old carrying around a ten-year-old as well; but you're carrying the eleven- and twelve-year-old around too, and all the other ages you passed through. Thus egotism is enormously multiplied. It grows less and less however if you detach yourself from the past by objectivizing it, so that it becomes more separate and distinct from you. This is the significant thing we should attend to.

(12 December 1918) [36]

On the concluding day of the year, before the new year begins, it seems to be an elementary need of all human souls to turn their thoughts to the transient nature of time. This elementary need makes us look back to examine ourselves and try to see what has approached our outward life, has come towards our soul during the year. We no doubt also look back to the progress we may have made, to the fruits of experiences which have arisen. When we conduct such a review then in a certain sense it sheds light on the feeling which shows us human life to be more or less valuable, more or less problematic or also more or less fulfilling. We can never just observe our life as a single, isolated human individual. Instead we feel compelled to consider it in connection with the rest of the world, the rest of humanity. If we are serious about our spiritual-scientific view of things, we will also in particular be aware of the need to repeatedly consider our relationship with the world at this turning point of the year, when one year ends and another begins.

(31 December 1918)[37]

We can look back on our own life for all sorts of reasons, with the most diverse aims. We can ask how this individual life unfolded from childhood until now. But we can also do it like this: rather than focusing so much on our own pleasure at one thing or another or how we experienced this or that, we can turn our gaze instead to the people who affected our lives in some way, as parents, siblings, friends, teachers and so on; and instead of ourselves, we can consider the nature of these people who intervened in our lives. By doing so it will appear for a while as if very little of how we are now is due to ourselves, and how much is due to what flowed into us from these others. If we honestly and authentically rehearse this kind of review of our life on an inner stage, our relationship to the world will actually become quite different. This review will leave behind a certain sense of things, certain feelings, as fertile seeds in us for real insight into human beings. Whoever repeatedly looks at his own nature and in this way perceives the part played in his own being by others—who may well have died now or no longer be in close connection with him—will also approach other people in a way that allows his individual, personal relationships to be informed by an imagination of the real nature of these other people. This is something which today and in future must arise in humanity as an inner, psychological and emotional impetus for human development and evolution.

(4 February 1919)[38]

4. Review exercise to comprehend karmic connections

It is possible to mature relatively quickly in one's capacity to comprehend karmic connections if one tries energetically, for a longer period, to allow to unfold in one's awareness, and increasingly in full awareness, what otherwise is not properly grasped: what is there in us but simply vanishes again. This is what happens with events we experience. What do people mostly do with the events and experiences that come towards them during the day? They only half-observe them. You can form an idea of this sort of semi-observation if you sit down in the afternoon or evening—and I advise you to do this—and ask yourself: 'What did I experience at 9.30 this morning?' Now try to recall whatever it was in every detail, as though the experience was simply fully present again at, say, 7.30 in the evening: as if it stood there before you, spiritually and artistically embodied and enacted before you. You will discover how much of the picture is missing, how much you failed to observe, how difficult this actually is. If you take a pen or pencil to write down this experience, you will soon start chewing on the pencil or pen instead, because you can't recall the details, and so you try to chew them out of the pencil instead.

Well, that is the initial task: to take an experience you have had and to conjure it vividly and clearly in your mind—not at the moment you have it, but later on—as if you were trying to paint it spiritually; to place it before your soul so that, if the experience involved someone speaking, you re-evoke this fully—the tone of voice, how the person put words together, in either an articulate or inarticulate way, and so on. Do this energetically, strongly, in other words form a vivid picture of what you experienced.

If you form a picture in this way of an experience you had during the day, when the astral body lifts away from the etheric and physical bodies during the following night it will occupy itself with this picture. In fact it is itself the bearer of this picture and is now forming and configuring it outside the body. The astral body takes this picture with it when it emerges from the body on the first night, and configures it outside the physical and etheric bodies.

This is the first step. We will go through these stages very carefully: the sleeping astral body configures the picture of the experience outside the physical and etheric body. Where does it do this? In the external ether. It is now outside in the external etheric world.

Now imagine a person: his physical and etheric bodies are lying in bed, and his astral body is outside him. We'll disregard the I for the time being. The astral body is outside, recreating this picture he formed; but it does so in the external ether, and the consequence of this is the following.

Consider that the astral body is outside and is now configuring this picture there [...]. All this happens in the external ether; and this external ether as it were encrusts with its own substance what is formed as picture in the astral body. In other words, here everywhere the external ether shapes the etheric form as a picture that has been so sharply formed in the mind's eye.

Now in the morning you come back into the physical and etheric body, and carry back into them what the external ether has made substantial. In other words: the sleeping astral body configures the picture of the experience outside the physical and etheric bodies, and the external ether penetrates the picture with its own substance.

You can imagine that this makes the picture stronger and that now, when the astral body comes back in, in the morning, with this greater substantiality, it can impress itself on the human being's etheric body. With forces derived from the external ether, it now impresses itself on your etheric body. So the second stage is this: the astral body impresses the picture upon your etheric body.

This is what happens on the first day and the first night. Now we arrive at day two, when you are once more involved in all of life's little preoccupations, in full, waking consciousness. But below the threshold of this consciousness, in the unconscious, the picture is settling down into the etheric body. And in the following night the etheric body, if not disturbed, elaborates this picture while the astral body is outside again. During the second night the picture is thus developed and elaborated by your own etheric body. The second stage is therefore this: the astral body impresses the picture upon the etheric body, and the etheric body elaborates this picture during the second night.

So now we have passed through the second day and the second night.

Now, if you go through this process, if you really do not neglect to continue to attend to the picture that you formed the day before—and you can continue to attend to it for a reason I will mention in a moment—then you will go on living with this picture.

What does it mean to continue to attend to it? You see, if you make an effort to form such a picture clearly, to really elaborate it sculpturally after you experienced it, on the first day, with its own characteristic, strongly delineated features, then you have exerted yourself spiritually. Something like this requires spiritual exertion. Forgive me if this sounds like a heavy hint—I am of course excluding all those present—but it has to be said that most people have no idea what spiritual exertion involves, for real spiritual exertion only arises through soul activity. If one simply allows the world to work upon one, allows thoughts to take their course without taking them in hand, no spiritual exertion is involved. Getting tired does not mean you have made spiritual exertions. You shouldn't think that getting tired from doing something means that you have exerted yourself spiritually. You can get tired while reading for example. But if you are not somehow co-productive as you read, if you merely allow the book's ideas to work upon you, you are not exerting yourself. In fact the opposite is true: someone who has really made spiritual exertions out of an inner soul activity may then reach for a book, doubtless a very interesting one, and by reading will then best 'sleep off' his spiritual exertions. Of course one can fall asleep over a book if one is tired, but this tiredness is no sign whatever of spiritual exertion.

A sign of having exerted yourself spiritually however is this: you get a sense that your brain is a little worn out, just as you feel an arm muscle that has been used in frequent lifting. Normal thinking does not make the brain participate and 'sympathize' in this way. But this effort is one you'll feel; and you might even notice on the first occasion, and on the second, third or tenth, that you get a mild headache. You won't feel tired or fall asleep—on the contrary: you won't be able to fall asleep, but are likely instead to get a slight headache. You shouldn't dismiss the headache as nothing but a nuisance but regard it as evidence of the fact that you have exerted your head.

Well, this will go on affecting you until you fall asleep. The next day, if you've really done this properly the day before, you will wake up with a sense that something, you're not quite sure what, is there in you! It's a sense that something wants something of you. Yes, you will see that it wasn't a matter of indifference that you formed this picture so clearly the day before, but that it has some significance. This picture has been transformed and now means that you have quite different feelings from those you usually have: the picture gives you quite specific feelings.

This will remain with you for the following day as the residual inner experience of the picture you formed. And what you feel there, which remains with you throughout the day, shows that the picture is now sinking down into the etheric body as I have described, and being absorbed by it.

After the next night, when you wake up again—in other words when you slip back in to your body again after these two days—you will probably find that you rediscover this picture within you somewhat reconfigured and transformed. You rediscover it within you, specifically when you wake up on the third day; and it will seem to you like a very real dream. But it has undergone a change and is not as it was. It will clothe itself in manifold pictures until it is something different. It will clothe itself in a picture as though some kind of spiritual beings were there who now bring this experience to you. And it will really strike you as if this experience you have had, which you formed into a picture, has now been brought close to you. If it was an experience with a person you will have the feeling, after going through this process, that your experience was not just via this person but that it has been somehow brought close to you: other, spiritual powers are involved, and they have brought it to you.

Now comes the following day. The picture will then be carried down from the etheric body into the physical body. On the following day the etheric body impresses this picture into the physical body. So we must say, as a third stage: the etheric body impresses the picture upon our physical body.

And now comes the next night. During the day you will again have attended to all life's little preoccupations but at the same time, below, this important thing is happening: the picture is being carried down into the physical body. This happens in your subconscious. Now when the next night comes this picture will be processed within the physical body, will be spiritualized there. First, during the day, this picture will descend into blood and nerve processes, but in the following night it will be spiritualized. Anyone who can perceive these things can see how this picture is processed by the physical body and then appears as a spiritually entirely altered picture. One can say that the physical body elaborates the picture during this next night.

Now this is something you need to imagine very accurately. The physical body really elaborates this picture spiritually. It spiritualizes it. When you have really done this, undergone this process, then, when you sleep, the physical body elaborates the whole thing, but not by retaining it in the physical body. A reconfiguration, a mighty, enlarged recreation of the picture arises everywhere out of the physical body. And when you get up again in the morning, this picture will stand there and you will float within it; it is really like a kind of cloud which contains you. You get up in the morning with this picture.

That's what happens on the third day and the third night. And then you get out of bed on the fourth day with this wholly transformed picture. You get up encompassed by and enclosed within this cloud. And if you really formed the picture on the first day with the necessary strength and clarity, if you were attentive to what your feelings gave you on the second day, you will now notice that your will is contained in this new picture. The will is within it, but it cannot express itself: it is as though chained. To use a somewhat extreme metaphor, it is as though one were an incredibly athletic runner and decided to run from London to Dover: I picture this and have the capacity for it. But at the moment I am about to start running, someone grips me and prevents me so that I stand there rigid: my whole will is raring to go but I cannot realize this will. That's about how it is.

When this experience develops—that you feel as if you're held in a vice, for this is what it feels like after the third night; when you wake up again and feel as if held tight in a vice— then, if you can attend to this, your will is transformed into seeing. It cannot act, but it enables you to see. It becomes an eye of soul; and the picture you got up with becomes substantial. And this is the connected event from your last life, or a past life, that causes this change to the picture you formed on the first day. Via this transformation through feeling and will, you receive the picture of the causative event from a former life.

(9 May 1924)[39]

5. Exercises in thinking backwards— illuminating the will

A third thing is necessary for religious insight.[40] One has to submerse oneself in the beings who reveal themselves pictorially in the inspired contents of knowledge. One achieves this by adding soul exercises of the will to the meditations so far described. For instance, one can try to picture processes that take a certain course in the physical world in reverse order, from the end back to the beginning. By doing so, through a will process we usually don't use in ordinary awareness, we can free soul life from the outward contents of the cosmos and instead immerse the soul in beings who reveal themselves in inspiration. Thus one arrives at true intuition, at community with the beings of a world of spirit. These experiences of intuition are reflected in our etheric and also physical nature, and in this reflection give rise to the content of religious awareness.

(GA 25, 1925)[41]

Our etheric body can grow substantially stronger if we do something else as well to improve our memory. I may have mentioned this before in another context, but I'd like to repeat it here, for these suggestions are helpful in combating all disorders which involve nervousness. We can do a very great deal to strengthen the etheric or life body if we run through things we know not just as we normally know them, but backwards. For instance, in school when children have to

learn a series of chronological events—battles or kings—with the corresponding dates. It is extremely beneficial if we don't just get children to learn these, or learn them ourselves, in the usual sequence but also learn them backwards, starting with the last and working back to the first. This is something extraordinarily important. If we do something like this thoroughly, we greatly strengthen our etheric body as well. Picturing whole plays in reverse, or stories or other reading matter, is of the very greatest importance for consolidating the etheric body.
(11 January 1912)[42]

In *Knowledge of the Higher Worlds* I suggest picturing things backwards sometimes, or reverse-reviewing them. Conducting a review of this kind means imagining from an opposite perspective events that take a particular course in the world: thinking them through in reverse.

By picturing things in reverse, alongside various other benefits we gradually make our mental powers capable of entering a world that runs in the opposite way from the physical world. This is the world of spirit. In many respects this world is the opposite of the physical world. I have pointed out previously that one cannot simply, abstractly, reverse what exists in the physical world; but the powers one develops must also include those connected with reverse picturing. What does this bring about? If people do not wish to become culturally desiccated, if they wish to find their way into a spiritual mode of seeing things, they will need to picture a reverse world. Spiritual awareness only begins where the life process or the sensory process is reversed and runs backwards. As we move into the future, therefore, people will have to get used to picturing or thinking things in reverse. They will access the world of spirit in this reverse thinking in the same way that they presently access the physical world in forwards thinking. Our ability to picture the physical world is due to the direction of our thinking sequences.

To continue in this vein—so far I have only led you from the human zodiac, the twelve sense spheres, through the life sphere of the planets—I would have to point you towards a quite different sort of thinking: a thinking in reverse.

[. . .]

It is easy to imagine that someone really fixed and frozen in contemporary modes of thinking would be appalled at the idea of thinking backwards, of picturing a world in reverse. But if this reverse world did not exist, there would be no consciousness at all. Yet consciousness itself is already a science of the spirit. This is something materialists deny.

[. . .]

Recently a curious book was published: *Kosmogonie* by Christian von Ehrenfels.[43] The book's first chapter is called 'The "Reversion", a Paradox of our Knowledge'. There Ehrenfels elaborates over many pages in the contemporary philosophic mode what it would be like if one were to try to imagine the other aspect, as it were the asymmetric aspect of the world: to think backwards. He really does get to this idea of thinking backwards, thinking in reverse. He tries to consider how to cope with this paradox, and conceives of this reverse thinking for special instances. I'd like to cite one example of this reverse thinking. He does not take a reverse sequence first but a forwards sequence:

In the normal world imagine that, due to humidity and frost, a lump is loosened from a compact cliff wall and that, when it thaws, the lump falls from the overhanging cliff face and shatters to many pieces below on a projection. Let us follow one of these pieces clattering downwards into a deep abyss, losing more splinters as it collides with stones, and at last coming to rest. In the process it has given out its whole kinetic energy in the form of heat conveyed to earth and rocks which it hit on the way down, and to the air which offered resistance to its motion. How would this—certainly not unusual—process unfold in the reversed world?

A stone lies below on the ground. Suddenly, apparently chaotic heat impulses from the earth beneath it are so strangely released that they give the stone a strong upwards impetus. The air offers it no resistance. On the contrary, due to strange, inherent heat transactions, it smoothes the stone's upward trajectory, parting before it by itself as the stone speeds straight up, and encourages this movement additionally with small yet purposeful warmth impulses. The stone collides with a projection of rock but it does not lose splinters nor is it slowed in its movement. On the contrary, another stone that by chance is hurled to the same spot at the same moment through accumulated warmth impulses is pressed against our stone, and the apparently irregular surfaces of these two pieces fit together so minutely and perfectly that the forces of cohesion are activated and the two stones grow to a compact mass. The larger lump, still impelled by apparently purposeful impulses of warmth, now, with still greater speed, continues its upward trajectory from the cliff projection it struck against.

The various bits of stone come back together in the same way that they splintered apart in the first scenario, and the lump rejoins the cliff face. He describes this all very precisely. In other words he thinks the process backwards. He cites various other such examples of thinking in reverse. [. . .]

A hare runs through the snow on a winter's morning, leaving tracks which the wind erases again in many places. By some south-facing slopes however, where the snow thaws in the sun and freezes again in the evening, the tracks can still be seen for weeks—until they vanish in the general thaw.

In the 'reversed world', the tracks of the hare would first form, not in their entirety but only here and there, initially as vague depressions in the frozen snow (or rather in the ice that gradually forms into loose snow); and then, after weeks, as those depressions gradually deepen and start looking more like paw-tracks, the trail would become visible in the intervening spaces—until at last the whole series of tracks appears; and now the hare arrives, his head facing backwards and the rear end facing in the direction of movement, running against the pull of his muscles, so artfully that one paw always falls exactly in each already formed paw-mark. But still greater wonders are to come: as soon as each paw lifts out of its track, the depression in the snow is completely and accurately filled with loose snow so that one cannot tell this place apart from its surroundings, and the path covered by the hare is soon a perfectly smooth surface as if it had always been so.

[. . .]

He makes strenuous efforts one can say, even if these are mental exertions: he exerts himself to grasp these reverse processes at least to some extent. He is certainly a thinker, it cannot be denied. It is logically quite possible to imagine this, but he says that it is not believable. In other words it contradicts his habitual train of thought. Ultimately this means that he cannot imagine a world of spirit. And now he concludes: 'But let us go further! Let us imagine what it would be like if experience were to require us to accept, as unavoidable reality, that such a "reversed world" exists.'

So the man tries to imagine, in the same way that he can see his hare outside him in the physical world, or its movements, what it would be like for him to see, in physical reality—which is the only reality for him—the reverse. Let's assume this is unavoidable experience: we go out one day and find a whole reversed world there:

> How would we relate to this world or attempt to interpret it? Despite the fact that we kept seeing it before our eyes as experience, the whole thought project we referred to, involving the reverse principle from the future backwards and the creation of form from nothing, would be one we must reject as absurd.

So he states that this would be terrible: we would be unable to think it and *should* not think it—and yet we would see it before our eyes! Thus he imagines the terrible nature of what he would have to see if he entered the spiritual world. For him this would be something terrible if it was imposed on him in the physical world as he pictures it:

> We would have no other choice but to regard this apparently spontaneous arising of forms (people, foxes or roses, etc.) as only apparently spontaneous, and in fact as caused by teleological, intentional accumulations of material particles that have been pre-calculated to initiate their directions of motion. This would apply likewise to the strange dynamic of their evolutionary convergence on parallel lines to ever less and less advanced forms.

In other words, he is thinking the whole thing backwards to Darwinian first principles at the beginning of the earth.

> But what would be the aim of this prefiguring, pre-calculated creative force? Can the sudden awakening of form and its gradual backwards development into non-form be an ultimate goal? No and again no! The aims of the whole must be the contrary of this.

And now he asks what such a world would look like to him if he really saw it. And his answer is this: 'This world I experienced would be the grotesque joke of an incomprehensible cosmic demon, to whom all is subject with the exception of knowledge.'

He retains his possession of knowledge, he says, for he cannot do otherwise. His knowledge consists of habits of thought which he cannot relinquish. But the world he would be compelled to see in reverse would be the grotesque drama staged by a cosmic demon, by the devil. He is afraid of what he would be compelled to regard as the devil. And here you can experience in a particular human soul what I have often said: fear of the world of spirit is what holds people back. He even expresses this, formulates it clearly: the moment we saw a physical world that was similar to the world of spirit, we would regard it as a paradox created by a devilish being. Thus he expresses his fear.

(13 August 1916)[44]

But the first thing we experience beyond the threshold is that there is a world in which time, as we view it, has no significance. We have to emerge from temporal concepts. This is why it is so useful if people who wish to prepare themselves to understand the world of spirit at least begin to picture things in reverse. Let us take a play that outwardly starts with Act I and progresses to Act V: we can start at the end and picture it backwards to the beginning of Act I. Likewise we can take a melody and imagine and feel it played backwards; also our experience of the day, in reverse sequence from the evening to the morning. By doing this we accustom our thinking to revoking time. In daily life we are used to picturing things happening in a sequence in which the second follows the first, the third follows the second, the fourth follows the third and so on; and our thinking invariably becomes a picture of the external course of events. But if we begin to think and feel backwards from the end of a sequence, then we are obliged to compel ourselves inwardly, and this compulsion is good, for it obliges us to depart from the ordinary world of the senses. Time runs from one to two, to three, four and so on, in this direction. If we think in the reverse direction—from the evening back to the morning instead of the usual way round, we are thinking against the flow of time and thus revoke time.

If we can extend such thinking so that we can think back in our life as far as we are able, this will be of very great benefit. Whoever does not emerge from the flow of time cannot enter the world of spirit.
(14 December 1919)[45]

[The sundering of will life from its daily preoccupation] can be brought about by freeing the will element that lives in thinking from the normal course and sequence that follows external physical circumstances. Will always works in thinking: thoughts are configured by the will; thought is just one aspect, for will is always interwoven with thoughts, and thoughts with will in our life of soul. We free the will from the normal course of events by, for instance, imagining something backwards. Say you are used to picturing the events of a play in the normal sequence from Act I to Act V. Instead, for once, you could picture it unfolding backwards from the last denouement back to the beginning. Then you can also try picturing outward events in reverse. For instance, in the evening you can think back through your day in as many short sequences as possible, from the evening back to the morning. You can go so far as to picture yourself climbing the stairs in reverse, so that you go backwards, from the top stair to the bottom, and so on.

The fact that we are used to thinking in the same direction as outward circumstances means that the will unfolding in our thinking plays a passive role. Thinking becomes inwardly active and filled with inner initiative if we free it from the outward course of events through exercises such as reverse thinking and thus make it self-reliant. We can enhance and strengthen what we achieve through such careful and energetic exercises by really rigorous self-observation—by observing what we do through our will as if we were standing beside ourselves and studying our own willed actions, one by one; or also by passing over into activity, undertaking exercises with the sole purpose of deciding to do something and then actually doing it precisely as we planned, with iron decisiveness. (In principle I aim to give exercises which not only free the will from outward circumstances but also from its body-bound condition, thus making the will autonomous and spiritualizing it.) In this way we develop our will in such a way that we experience our soul life—which instigates the will—outside of the body. This is a significant experience. But only by this means do we first gain insight into the nature of the will. In normal life the will is bound to our organs. We see its motions when we move our limbs. Only through our life of thought do we observe the resulting processes, the effects of our will. But when we free the will from corporeality, we gain insight into its nature, experiencing it intrinsically, becoming entirely one with it. Then it is permeated by an enhancement of the power that is otherwise also tied to our physical organism: it is permeated by the power of love. And this devotional element in the psyche that, I would say, we meet in love as dark or emotional will life then acquires a transparent, bright clarity.

(17 January 1922)[46]

I would like to accentuate a few of the wide range of will exercises I have described in my books. For example, one can exercise the will by schooling it through thinking. Our life of soul is so constituted that the separate capacities of thinking, feeling and will which we distinguish in abstract terms when we try to characterize the psyche are in reality not so far removed from each other. One faculty plays into the other. The will plays into thinking when we connect thoughts and disconnect them again, and so forth. Now there is a will exercise which involves voluntarily thinking backwards what one is otherwise accustomed to think forwards, in line with external facts. For example, you can think through a play in reverse, from Act V to Act I—and thus from the closing events to the initial ones in Act I. Or you can go through a poem backwards, thinking and feeling your way from the last line to the first. Another exercise of particular benefit is to think through parts of one's day in the evening in reverse, as vividly as possible, starting with the last event of the evening and working back to the morning. In doing this you should treat each small sequence as atomistically as possible, even going so far as to imagine how you climbed the stairs in reverse, backwards from the top stair to the bottom, and so on. And the more you form thoughts in this unusual way, not bound to the circumstances themselves, the more you free the will—which is used to adapting passively to outward circumstances—from these outward events and also from physical corporeality. Once one has done such exercises one can also find support in others, which I would call self-observation and self-schooling exercises. Here you should get to the stage of being able to evaluate your own actions and will impulses from without, just as one would objectively assess the actions and will impulses of another person. In relation to one's own will decisions and actions one has to become more or less one's own, objective observer.

But we have to go still further. When we consider our lives we know that we have changed over the years. Each of us knows that we were different ten years ago as regards our whole psychological mood and state of soul. But what has become of us during the years is what life itself, outer reality, has made of us. We just need to consider these things without prejudice, seeing how we passively give ourselves up to outer reality. To find our way into higher worlds we can practise active self-schooling. We can take our own schooling in hand by deciding to relinquish a certain habit. We can then use all our powers to relinquish this habit or to develop a different quality or characteristic. If we succeed in acquiring by our own self-discipline what otherwise only life gives us, then we also gradually manage to free the will from physical corporeality.

(24 January 1922)[47]

In relation to the will aspect this is the case: the initiate of ancient times tried, as I said, to render his will organization rigid. This enabled him in turn to perceive the soul and spirit that are otherwise sucked up by the will organization—in other words to perceive what still lived in him from pre-birth existence. When the body is rigidified, it no longer sucks up the soul and spirit; and the latter is then revealed as autonomous entity. As modern initiates we do not do this. We proceed in a different way. Instead, we strengthen the will by transforming the power of will as I have described elsewhere. It would be quite wrong to induce cataleptic states as was done to ancient initiates through causing shock, terror or fear. For modern human beings with a strongly developed intellectualism, this would lead to a wholly pathological condition, and must not be done. By means of reverse sequence exercises, in contrast—where, instead of thinking forwards in the usual way one goes through one's experiences in reverse, for instance from the evening back to the morning—or also other will exercises, the will can be transformed in a way that I can characterize as follows.

Consider the human eye. What form and structure does it need to enable us to see? If we develop a cataract, the material of the eye asserts itself, cloaking it with matter and becoming opaque. The eye has to be selfless and selflessly incorporated into the organism if we are to use it for proper sight: it has to be transparent. Our organism is certainly not transparent for the will. I have often described this to you. We can have the idea, let us say, that we are going to move our arm or hand. We form this thought: I'm going to lift my hand or arm. But what occurs in our organism when this thought shoots over into it and realizes it is as shrouded in darkness as the events that occur between falling asleep and waking up again. All we see is the raised arm or hand, and gain an idea from this in turn. Initial idea and concluding idea close the circle, but what lies in between these two is a state of sleep. The will unfolds in the unconscious in the same way that the state of sleep unfolds there. We really can say that our organism is as opaque for the will's perception in ordinary consciousness as an eye with a cataract is opaque for vision.

Naturally I do not mean that the human organism is therefore sick. For ordinary, practical life the organism has to be opaque, and that is its normal state. But for higher knowledge to develop it cannot remain so. It has to become transparent for soul and spirit, and this is achieved through the will exercises. The organism becomes transparent for us so that we no longer look down into a vague, hidden realm when will actions occur, but this will becomes instead as selfless as the eye within the organism if we are to see outward things properly. Just as the eye itself is transparent, so the organism becomes transparent in a soul-spiritual sense: the whole organism becomes a sense organ. By this means, via the aspect of will, we can objectively perceive spiritual beings in the same way that we perceive external objects through the outward eye. In other words, the will exercises are not intended to rigidify the body so that the spirit becomes free, but instead they aim to develop the soul and spirit in such a way that these can see through the body. This is an important difference. We can only see into the world of spirit if we look through ourselves. Just as we only perceive outward objects with our eyes by looking through the eyes, so we cannot see into the world of spirit directly but only by looking through ourselves.

This is the other aspect, of self-development via the will. In modern times all self-development depends on first strengthening thinking so that it becomes independent of the brain, and secondly configuring the will so that the whole human being becomes transparent. We can't gaze into the world of spirit through pie-in-the-sky, just as little as we can see the world of colours without eyes. We have to look through ourselves, and this can be done via the will exercises.

(12 February 1922)[48]

I would now like to briefly describe how one can gradually carry the power of thinking into the will, as I have said is the case with the concentration exercises. Let's start with a straightforward example that anybody can do every day. We sit down calmly and think about what we experienced during the day—but not starting in the morning and surveying the day's events as they occurred in chronological sequence. Instead we review our day by starting with the latest experiences in the evening, and working our way back to earlier ones in the morning. We work our way back in sequences that are as short as possible. To begin with it is fine just to take a single episode from the day, and later the memory tableau will suggest and arrange itself. What is important is this: we are accustomed to giving our thinking quite passively over to the outward course of events, always conceiving what happened later as succeeding what occurred earlier. This only weakly develops the will through thinking. We strengthen the will by proceeding in the opposite direction, freeing or sundering thinking from the course of outward events by picturing them in reverse. We practise our will-power by feeling events backwards from the end to the beginning. In the same way one can think a melody backwards, or picture the course of a play from the last act to the first. The important thing here is to invoke a strong will to detach ourselves from the external sequence of events. This strengthens the will and develops the power in us to drive thinking into the will in the same way that we drove will into thinking in the concentration and meditation exercises. I have described this in more detail in the books I mentioned.[49]

I would like to make this clearer with a few examples. You can undertake this kind of self-education of the will with full energy, not only giving yourself up to life's external aspects—to what education and environment have made of you—but instead pursuing a self-education based on mature insight, taking yourself in hand fully to the extent that you relinquish a habit, say, and instead acquire something else in its place through such exercises extending over years. If you say to yourself that simply through the power of your thinking, the power of your will living in your life of thinking, you will try to develop in yourself a particular characteristic that you don't at present possess, and make it into a lasting quality, this might take seven years of practice. And if we repeatedly do such a thing, from decade to decade, if we keep repeating it, this will strengthen our will. And there are various other will exercises too which likewise enable us to enter the world of spirit from another direction.

But how does our consciousness relate to these will impulses? We can understand this in the following way. I have an impulse of will when I raise my hand or arm. This will impulse submerges itself in the depths of my being, and is removed from normal waking consciousness in the same way that I lose awareness when I sleep. We dream in our feelings as it were, but are asleep in our will impulses. So we can say that in a certain sense our souls are opaque. Just as this or that object appears to us opaque to physical light, so our body is opaque in relation to the will. We cannot look into the will whereas we can see with the physical eye because it is transparent. If we have a cataract disorder, we can no longer see properly. I do not mean at all that we are 'sick' in ordinary life as regards our physical organism. Anthroposophy has no wish to engage in false asceticism. But if we were to reach the stage of rendering the body transparent—not in a physical sense of course, but in terms of soul perception—we would also really come to the point of seeing how our thoughts stream into the physical organism's will impulses. We would be able to follow and gain perception of our will impulses because our physical organism would then be transparent. Similarly we gain perception of ourselves as will beings and at the same time gaze into the spiritual world of will, to which we belong, when we see into that externality which we render transparent through will exercises. For someone who achieves a stage of knowledge where the physical body becomes transparent—since the will is seen and observed—this physical body disappears initially for his gaze and vision; and if he wishes to see ever further and is strengthened to do so in the way described he arrives in vision at the moment of death, forms a picture of that moment when we give back our physical body to the earth and pass through the gates of death with our soul and spirit. This picture of passing through the gate of death is one we have before us when we reach the stage of rendering our physical body transparent so as to gaze into the spiritual realm. Then we understand what this physical body no longer possesses, and that we are not only gazing into the world of spirit but actually living into it, entering it. This stage of perception is that of intuitive knowledge, true intuitive knowledge. This level gives us a vision of immortality.

(14 April 1922)[50]

Now I'd like to describe a simple will exercise as specific example, so that you can study the principle involved here. In ordinary life we are used to thinking in correspondence with the course of mundane things. We allow whatever happens to approach us in the way it happens. What happened earlier to us we think of as earlier, and what happened later, as later. And even if we do not necessarily think chronologically in more logical thought, nevertheless the effort is there in the background to adhere to the course of external reality. But to become more practised in the relationships of soul-spiritual forces, we need to free ourselves from the external course of events. There is a good exercise for this, which is at the same time a will exercise: we can try to re-experience our day— which in outward reality proceeds from the morning to the evening—in reverse, from the evening back to the morning, and as we do so we can try as far as possible to enter into small details.

Let's assume that in reviewing our day we recall climbing a flight of stairs. We can imagine ourselves at the top of the stairs, then see ourselves on the top stair but one, and so on downwards or backwards. To begin with we will only be able to picture distinct episodes from our daily life in this way, going back from six in the evening to three, from midday to nine in the morning and so on, until we arrive at the moment we first woke up. But we will gradually acquire a kind of technique by means of which we will in fact be able to allow the day to pass before us in pictures, in a reverse tableau, either on the evening of the same day or on the following morning. When we are able—and this is what counts—to free our thinking entirely from the way in which reality unfolds, in three dimensions, then we will see how this enormously strengthens our will. We will also achieve this if we become able to feel a melody in reverse, or to picture a play of five acts backwards from the fifth to the fourth act and so on, back to the beginning of the play. All these things strengthen the will by inwardly consolidating it and outwardly freeing it from its sensory attachment to outward events.

To this can be added other exercises such as those I suggested in previous lectures: examining this or that habit which we have. We can firmly undertake to replace it within a couple of years with a different habit, and then apply iron will to do so. Just as an example, each of us has his own distinct handwriting. If we make efforts to acquire a different handwriting, which does not in the least resemble our original hand, this will require considerable inner effort. The second handwriting must become just as habitual and natural to us as the first was. This is a comparatively trivial thing, and merely an example. There are many areas where we can change the whole fundamental tenor of our soul life through our own energetic efforts. By doing so we gradually not only internalize the world of spirit in ourselves as inspiration, but really also immerse ourselves in other spiritual beings outside us with our now body-free spirit. Real spiritual perception is in fact an immersion in the beings who spiritually surround us when we look upon physical things. If we wish to perceive spiritual things we first have to emerge from ourselves. I have described this. But then we must also acquire the capacity, in turn, to enter deeply into things and beings.

We can only do this after undertaking the kinds of initiation exercises I have just described, in which we are no longer disturbed by our own body but can instead submerge ourselves in the spiritual aspect of things. Then, for instance, the colours of flowers no longer appear to us as such, but we immerse ourselves in the colours themselves—so that we no longer see the flowers as merely coloured but see them acquiring colour; then we know that the cornflower growing by the wayside is not only blue when we look at it, but that we can inwardly immerse ourselves in the blossom and participate in the blue-growing process. We are then intuitively participating in this process and, from that starting point, can extend our spiritual insight ever further.
(20 August 1922)[51]

We need to develop meditative life through soul exercises in order to gain understanding of religious experience. But this meditative life, these soul exercises must now be extended to the human will. So far, I have primarily described the type of soul exercises that are distinguished by a special development of thinking. But now soul life, in so far as it is manifest in the will, must be freed in the spiritual researcher from the life of the physical organism and the etheric organism. This can be done by using the will in a way it is not normally used. Let me illustrate what I mean with an example.

You can try to picture events in the outer world that you usually trace in their chronological sequence—first what happened earlier, then what happened later—in reverse order, first taking what happened most recently, then what happened immediately before that and backwards to the beginning. By making this will exertion the soul undertakes something it does not usually do in ordinary life. In ordinary consciousness we follow the outward course of events with the will living in our thinking. By means of this reverse thinking, which is different from the way things unfold in the natural world, we can free the will from the physical and etheric organism, thus connecting the will, which is anyway only a reflection of the astral organism, with this same astral organism. And since, through the other forms of meditation, the astral body is lifted out of the physical and etheric organism, by this means one raises the will as well from the physical organism into the external spiritual world. By driving the will in our astral body out of our own organism, we also take what is in fact the spirit man or the I out of the physical and etheric organism, so that we can now live with our I and astral organism in the spiritual world together with spiritual beings dwelling there. In the physical world we live alone in our own physical body; now, by developing our life of soul in the way I have described, we learn to live in the external spiritual world in community with all the beings that have first revealed themselves in imagination and inspiration. By this means we can attain a life in the world of spirit that is independent of our corporeality.

We can further enhance such exercises by exerting the will in a different way. The more effort we have to expend to develop the will, the better it is for our capacity to experience the spiritual world outside the physical and etheric organism.

We can transform habits by intentionally undertaking to reconfigure this or that habit we may have had for years. Through energetic application of will we can try to transform this habit within four, five or ten years so that we appear to others to be a changed and different person, at least as regards the original habit. These may be small, insignificant habits, perhaps even so trivial that they carry on in us without us being very aware of them. If one works on these, they are actually the most suitable for the kind of supersensible insights and perception that I have been describing. For instance, people have their own particular type of hand-writing style. Now we can decide energetically to acquire a different kind of handwriting from the one habitual to us, which we have developed from childhood on. If we devote ourselves for years to such will exercises, the soul will ulti-mately be strong enough to live in the external spiritual world, outside the physical and etheric organism, with spiritual beings—with human souls either before they des-cend to physical existence or when, after they have passed through death, they dwell in the world of spirit before they return again to physical existence; or also with the beings of spirit who only dwell in the spiritual world, and do not, unlike human beings, ever clothe themselves in an etheric and physical organism.

In this way we will come to the point of living as soul and spirit in the world where we can experience what con-stitutes religious consciousness. [...] We thus reach the third stage of supersensible knowledge, where true intui-tion develops.

(7 September 1922)[52]

Modern people have to take their will directly in hand. In *Knowledge of the Higher Worlds* and *Occult Science* you will find a whole range of exercises that help with self-schooling and self-development, above all in relation to the will. Here I just want to mention a few.

We are used to our thinking as it were accompanying the course of outward events in a chronological sequence. But we can alter this, for example by picturing what we experience last in the day, in the evening, then working back through the day in reverse, back to the morning. Thus we place the natural sequence of events before us in reverse order. By doing so we sunder ourselves with our thinking— which normally adheres to natural sequences proceeding from the earlier to the later—from this natural progression. We think contrary to the natural course of things, and by this means the will in thinking is strengthened. This is particularly true if we pay close attention to small, trivial things.

For instance, imagine you climbed a staircase: instead of standing on the bottom step, picture yourself on the top step, then see the whole stair-climbing sequence as a descent. Thus you free yourself from the actual experience, picturing it in reverse. This strengthens the will contained in thinking. I can also strengthen this will by taking my self-education in hand, saying to myself that I will change this or that habit. I undertake to change this habit, in three years, say, so that by then I will have replaced it with a quite different habit. Thus there are hundreds and thousands of exercises that can directly work to reconfigure the will, so that it detaches and frees itself from what mere corporeality imposes on it.

In this way the modern human being does something

similar to what ancient people did by assuming certain bodily positions. For the reasons mentioned we cannot go back to these ancient exercises. By doing what I suggest, the modern human being can increasingly bring his supersensible aspect into relationship with the supersensible aspect of the world. *(1 November 1922)*[53]

The first thing we must learn in order to enter the world of spirit is to think properly. How to do so is something we will consider further—it is a complex issue. Today we must first establish what is involved. The first thing necessary is an entirely self-reliant thinking. To achieve this we have to break with many things that are implicit in modern education, which inculcates a non-autonomous thinking derived from Latin. [...]

The second thing we need to do is to learn not to live merely in the present moment but to be able to return repeatedly to the life we have led since childhood. You see, if you wish to penetrate into the world of spirit you have to try to look back at how you were at the age, say, of twelve. What did you do at that age? And this mustn't be done in a superficial, external way, but in small, specific detail. For instance, there is nothing more useful than to picture yourself vividly at the age of twelve in a particular setting. Perhaps there was a pile of stones on the road and you climbed it and tumbled down. Or there was a hazelnut bush, and you took your pocket-knife and cut branches from it, and cut your finger. Really, vividly seeing what you yourself did enables you not to live merely in the present. If you think as people have learned to do nowadays, you are thinking with your present physical body. But if you go back to what you were at the age of twelve, you cannot think with your physical body of that time for it no longer exists—the physical body renews itself every seven years as I've said before—and you have to think with your etheric body instead. That is why you invoke this etheric body when you think back to what happened when you were twelve or fourteen, and thereby you enter into inner activity.

There is a particular way of acquiring a different mode of thinking from the usual one. How do you usually think? We met here today at nine o'clock, and I started to read out to you the questions that had been handed in to me.[54] I made all kinds of observations, and then we arrived at the idea of the need to look back to an earlier stage of our lives, when we were twelve or fourteen. Now when you get home, if you feel interested in thinking through what we have discussed, you can do so. Most people do this: they think through what was discussed. But you can also do this in a different way. You can ask yourself: What was the last thing he said? The last thing he mentioned was that one should look back to oneself at a younger age, to when one was twelve or fourteen. Before that he spoke of the need to have a free, autonomous thinking. Before that he talked about how Latin has gradually come to influence education. Prior to that he spoke of how someone who has not been mentally well for a while can look back and say that in fact he learned or experienced something special during this period. Then, going back further, he spoke of how the inner human being does not become mentally ill, but that only the body becomes sick. In this way you could work your way back through the whole lecture in reverse.

Of course, in the outer world things do not run in reverse! I could perhaps have delivered my lecture backwards, but then you would not understand it, for the usual thing is to start at the beginning and build things up in such a way that understanding can gradually develop. But once one has understood, one can also think it backwards. Yet facts and circumstances do not unfold in reverse! So I am freeing and detaching myself from facts and circumstances. Thinking backwards, at odds with chronological sequence, requires a certain strength: I have to be inwardly active. Just as someone who looks through a telescope must learn to handle it, so someone who wishes to look into the world of spirit must often think in reverse, repeatedly think in reverse. Then a time will come when he realizes that he can enter the world of spirit.

From this you can once again see that, all through your life, you have accustomed your physical body to thinking forwards. If you now start thinking backwards your physical body will not be involved, and instead something remarkable happens. This is the first piece of advice to give to those who repeatedly ask 'How do I enter the world of spirit?' You can also find this in *Knowledge of the Higher Worlds*. They should learn at least to work backwards through the events of each day, and then apply this reverse thinking to other things too. Initially people have learned only to think physically, with their physical body. Now they make efforts to think backwards but they have learned only to think with their physical body so far, not with their etheric body. And at this point the etheric body goes on strike—it calls a general strike! And if people did not fall asleep so quickly when thinking backwards, they would know that by starting to think in reverse they inevitably arrive in the world of spirit. At the moment vision would otherwise begin, people fall asleep because the exertion is too great. So one needs the great good will and full strength not to fall asleep at this point. And this requires patience. It may sometimes take years; one just has to have patience.

(28 June 1923)[55]

The third step in higher knowledge that is necessary for entering the region of intuition can only be achieved by developing to the fullest extent a particular inner capacity. In today's materialistic culture this is not regarded in any way as a power of cognition. Only by developing and spiritualizing love to the fullest extent can we achieve what manifests in intuition. It must become possible for people to make the capacity of love into a power of cognition. We prepare ourselves well for this spiritualized capacity of love if we free ourselves to some degree from our attachment to outward things: if, for instance, we regularly practise picturing things we have experienced not in the sequence they happened but in reverse.

With our passive thinking we are subject to events in the world somewhat like slaves. When we form thoughts, as I said yesterday, we are used to thinking first what happened first, and thinking afterwards what happened afterwards. When we watch a play, the first act comes first, followed by the second, third, fourth and fifth. But if we can start at the end of the play, then picture what happens at the beginning of Act V, then go backwards to Act IV, and so on through the third and second acts to the beginning, we free ourselves entirely from the world's external sequence. We engage in reverse thinking or picturing. This is not the way of the world. We have to make a purely inner exertion to think backwards, and this effort is significant. By doing so we free our soul from the reins that otherwise continually pull on us, and thereby we bring our inner, soul-spiritual experience gradually to the point where it can really sunder itself from the corporeal and also from the etheric.

A good way to prepare for this sundering is to try to picture our experiences of the day's events in reverse each evening: first what we experienced last of all, then working back through the day—but if possible also thinking through the details of each smaller sequence in reverse, for instance picturing backwards how we climbed the stairs; thinking ourselves first at the top of the stairs then on the penultimate step, the third from the top and so on, conceiving in reverse what we actually accomplished forwards.

You may say that so many things happen each day that this will take a long time. Well, try first taking a very short sequence, going up and downstairs in reverse: just up and down. By doing this you acquire an inner flexibility so that after a while you will really be able to picture the whole sequence of the day, in reverse, in three or four minutes. Thereby you have in fact only accomplished half—basically the negative half—of what is needed to enhance your capacities and develop the spiritualized power of love. This capacity must develop to the point where you lovingly accompany every change in the growth of a plant. Normally one only observes the growth of a plant as it unfolds spatially—one does not accompany it inwardly. You must try to accompany every tiny change apparent in a growing plant. Immerse yourself in the plant, becoming the plant with your soul so that you yourself grow, blossom and bear fruit; immerse yourself in it entirely in this way so that the plant becomes as valuable to you as yourself. Then ascend in the same way to picturing the animal realm, and descend to the mineral realm likewise, sensing how the mineral shapes itself into crystalline form, and developing as it were an inner sense of well-being at the way the crystal forms surfaces, edges and angles—a sense of inner well-being as you observe these surfaces, edges and angles. And, as the mineral is split and fissured, you should try to feel something like a sense of pain quivering through your being. In this way you develop sympathy or 'fellow feeling'—and not just this but also 'fellow will' in your soul—with all natural occurrences.

This must be preceded by a real capacity for love that encompasses all human beings. You won't be able to properly love nature in the way described if you do not first develop the capacity to love all human beings. Once you have achieved this kind of loving insight into human beings and all nature then what is initially perceptible as the colours of the human aura, in the musical tones of the spheres, will fill out and assume the configurations of actual spiritual beings. *(20 August 1923)*[56]

6. The review and kamaloka

But if you wish to properly interpret what, after death, succeeds this tableau of your past life on earth, you will need another type of exercise.

During life and also in mainstream science, we usually give ourselves—our thoughts, feelings and will impulses—passively to the external world. We advance in a forwards linearity with the outer world. We experience yesterday as preceding today, which in turn is followed by tomorrow. And our soul life, too, the inner mirroring that unfolds in thought, feeling and will, adheres to the outward course of time as ongoing, natural experience. This gives us a certain kind of support for ordinary thinking, and for ordinary feeling too. But by giving ourselves passively in this way to the outward trajectory of time alone, we cannot strengthen our thinking to the extent necessary for supersensible research. We have to practise something else additionally and try, if I may put it like this, to think backwards. When the day is over we can review all that we have seen by allowing the day's events to pass before us in reverse sequence, from the evening to the morning: not in thoughts, nor with a critical stance, but as though imagining it in pictures, vividly—as though we once again see what happened. We need to acquire a certain facility in this reverse picturing. It is relatively easy to picture larger portions of the day in reverse; but really we need to picture small portions in reverse: tiny sequences that compose the day. Then one can pass on to other exercises, perhaps supporting this process by, let us say, picturing a play backwards from the fifth to the first act, or inwardly experiencing a melody backwards from the end to the beginning, hearing it soul-spiritually as it were. And then one can arrive at the point of viewing one's life in memory—this is now something different from the tableau I described—by recalling in reverse all that one has experienced, conjuring it up before the soul in an imaginative, pictorial way. By doing such exercises we free thinking from the outward course of events. We have to overcome the deeply rooted habit of following the outward course of time with our thinking, sensing and feeling. By thinking backwards and doing so energetically, we become able to draw on a much greater and stronger power of thought than we need for merely passive thinking. This substantially strengthens our thinking capacity.

And by doing this we discover something that no doubt sounds paradoxical to ordinary consciousness and cognition. Just as we perceive the sensory world through thinking and picturing that flows in time's sequential direction, so we gradually come to perceive the world of spirit by freeing our thinking from the outward course of events. And at the same time we acquire an additional capacity too: to observe the further experience that succeeds the life tableau we experience for several days after death and, from the perspective I have described, to interpret it properly. Like a person after death, after he has seen the panorama of his life spread before him, we can now look backwards, in reverse sequence, on our experiences, and see them in real and vivid pictures. You can say that we experience the soul world before the spirit world. In a process that takes place more quickly than our actual life between birth and death, after death we live backwards through our life until we reach the moment of our birth. The capacity to understand what we see there is one we can acquire through these exercises in reverse thinking. And now we can gain a clearer sense of how, after death, in this life of soul proceeding in reverse, we experience all that happened to us during our earthly life in a physical body. The only difference is that we now experience it in soul form, and gain understanding and perception of all that we did to impede our moral progress. As time unfurls in reverse, we can review all that we must now, from a higher perspective, wish should be different in our life. We can see how we remained imperfect through moral deficiencies. But since we experience this in a living, vivid way, it does not remain a thought only. In the life of soul that runs backwards, or develops backwards in this way, thoughts do not remain abstract—abstract thoughts are relinquished at death—but instead a *power* of thought develops. This power develops as the impetus to make redress in some way, in one's next life— in some way to experience the opposite of what now rises as pictures before the soul. In the soul there unfolds something which in our next life will appear as subconscious longings for this or that experience. Through this life experienced in reverse there develops a longing, in our next life, to seek a compensating set of circumstances for everything we have undergone. In this reverse development we can experience the germ of what we will bring with us unconsciously to our next birth [...].

(29 November 1921)[57]

Yes, this is true: every night we live back through our waking life. Some do so quicker, others more slowly—maybe in five minutes or maybe just one. These things are governed by quite different temporal relationships than apply to outward earthly life. But if we consider what happens in an ordinary night, imagination and inspiration can give us perception of the experiences of the I and astral body. These do indeed re-experience in reverse all that has been undergone since you last woke up to the physical world. Every night we relive the day, but in reverse sequence. Each night we live through what we did and experienced last, in the evening, then what happened somewhat earlier, then what occurred still earlier, and then what lies still further back in the day. In reverse sequence we relive our day's experiences, and usually we wake up when we reach the morning.

You might object that people are often woken up by some noise or other. But time relationships are different in sleep. Imagine that you go to bed at a decent time, let's say at eleven, and then sleep soundly until three in the morning; at which point let's say that you have gone back, in reverse order, to what happened the day before at about ten in the morning—and then a noise wakes you up. If this happens you just swiftly re-experience the rest of the day backwards as you wake up. This can happen in moments. What remains always unfolds very quickly in such a case, though otherwise it might take hours. Time relationships are different when you sleep: time can be compressed. Each time we fall asleep we go backwards through all we experienced during our last waking period. We do not merely observe it in a detached way, but a full moral evaluation of what we underwent mingles with it.

We become our own moral judge, you can say, as we live backwards through what we experienced. And when, on awakening, we have completed this reliving in reverse, then in a certain sense we have passed judgement on ourselves. Each morning, on awakening, after reliving in reverse what we accomplished the day before, we appraise ourselves as being of this or that worth. But this process of the soul and spirit that unfolds each night—and thus normally takes up a third of our life—is an unconscious one. The soul relives each day of our life in reverse sequence, though faster than the original experience since we only spend about a third of our life asleep.

When eventually we pass through the gate of death after laying aside the physical body, what I have called the etheric body or body of formative forces gradually separates over a few days from the I and astral body. This separation is such that after passing through the gate of death we feel how our thoughts—which we previously regarded as something merely within ourselves—are in fact realities that increasingly spread out. Two or three days after death we feel that we actually consist of thoughts, but that these thoughts are diffusing and spreading outwards. As a thought being we grow ever more expansive, and eventually this whole thought being diffuses into the cosmos. But as the thought being, or in other words the etheric body, dissolves into the cosmos, what we experienced otherwise than through our ordinary consciousness comes increasingly into focus.

By three days after death, everything we thought or pictured in a waking state has dissipated. This is the case and we shouldn't close our eyes to it. The content of our conscious life on earth evaporates three days after death. But as what is so important to us, so significant during our earthly life, fades away within three days after death, there rises out of our inner being a memory that was not there before—of all that we underwent in reverse sequence during the nights, between falling asleep and waking up again. The waking life of day consciousness fades away, and to the same extent that it does so the sum of experiences we underwent during the night rises from our inner being. Our daytime experiences are contained there too, but in reverse order, and every detail is interwoven with a moral feeling.

Now remember that we remain at the beginning of life with the real I and astral body,[58] but what we acquire as mirror images with the physical body, however old we have become, evaporates with the etheric body. What we did not see at all during our earthly life, our nightly experiences, surfaces in us now as new content. After the etheric body has dissipated after three days, then we feel ourselves really to be at the end of our life on earth. If we die, say, on 16 May 1923, through the fact that all our nightly experiences now surface as if from the darkness, we feel ourselves borne to the end of our earthly life—but with the simultaneous inclination to go back through it. And now we relive the time we always slept through: we go back through it, night by night, and this takes up about a third of the time our whole life took.

The diverse religions describe this as purgatory or kama-loka etc.[59] We relive our life on earth in the way we relived it unconsciously each night, until we arrive back at the very beginning of our life. We have to go back to the beginning of our life on earth. The wheel of life must turn, and return to its beginning. This is what happens. Three days after death our waking experiences fly away from us. Then, in a period amounting to a third of our life, we pass back through it in reverse and in this process become fully aware of our worth as a human being. What we experienced unconsciously each night now surfaces in full awareness after we have laid aside our etheric body.

(16 May 1923)[60]

7. The review and education

In the case of sluggish thinking, as in class 3, you can for example take a phrase such as 'The tree grows green' and turn it round to get 'Green grows the tree' and so forth, so that the children have to quickly reverse the thought.
(1 January 1920)[61]

In the case of children who steal, it is good to get them to recall scenes that they experienced when they were younger: seven-year-olds can look back to experiences when they were five, and ten-year-olds to experiences when they were seven. And it is good to get them used to moving on to different experiences after a fortnight. Then things will quickly improve. If you do nothing these conditions get worse, and can deteriorate into kleptomania. Something like kleptomania can later emerge.

Whatever consolidates the will is particularly effective for such things; and recalling memories by getting them to look back weeks, months or years consolidates the will.

[...]

However there are also children who have a poor memory—who cannot remember today what they did yesterday. Then you have to strengthen their memory by getting them to picture things backwards.

[...]

There is scarcely any other way to improve the memory than by trying to get children to picture something backwards. You can get them to reverse the sentence 'The father reads the book': 'Book the reads father the'; and do it so that they think pictorially. Or get them to speak number sequences in reverse: 4673 thus becomes 3764. Or they can recite the hardness scale[*] forwards and backwards.

Once children have learned little poems you can also get them to say these backwards, word by word. It is also good to do the speech exercises backwards. This is a technique one must use if children display a very poor memory.
(8 March 1920)[62]

Question: Is it helpful to get children to do the review exercise as early as the age of five or six?
Rudolf Steiner: I don't know what prompted this question. I don't know, either, if the question is based on experience. It seems to be, for here it is. I'm actually surprised at this question, for I would have thought that the nonsense of getting children to practise the review would not occur. As you know from my books, especially *Knowledge of the Higher Worlds,* the review exercise is practised for spiritual development, for gradually coming to real spiritual perception. You can easily gain a sense of the deeply incisive effect of such review if you consider that the other kind of thinking, that runs chronologically forwards in line with natural phenomena, is what informs ordinary consciousness. If we

---

[*]The Mohs scale of mineral hardness characterizes the scratch resistance of various minerals through the ability of a harder material to scratch a softer material. It was created in 1812 by the German mineralogist Friedrich Mohs.

make a certain inner exertion to review the day, allowing its events to pass before us in reverse, from the evening to the morning, we pull ourselves free from this ordinary thinking, picturing and experiencing of things. We pull ourselves free. And by engaging in this radically opposite activity, we gradually become able to emancipate the soul and spirit. Such practice forms a support that enables us to progress spiritually.

Now the question might have meant—it is not clear—that such an exercise suited for spiritual development at a later age might be adapted for children. This would simply be nonsense, for it would introduce complete disorder into the relationship in the child between his soul-spirit and physical-etheric. You would soon see the dire consequences of this. Allowing children to do such an exercise would mean very prematurely sundering what corresponds in them to thinking, feeling and will, thus bringing such disorder into the child's whole soul-spiritual-physical organization that you would—deliberately—develop childhood dementia in him, a kind of dementia praecox. If such things are to be countenanced at all, then one really has to know that they must not be used in a dilettante fashion, and particularly not for a child aged five or six. It would be absolute nonsense to do anything like this before puberty. If the question means getting the child to look back on the events of the day, then at least it should not be taken to extremes. It can sometimes be necessary, for one reason or another, for the child to remember a bit of bad behaviour or something joyful he experienced, but developing a certain hypochondria in the child through repeated review is certainly a kind of nonsense, albeit a small piece of nonsense compared—if that was what was meant—with getting the child to do spiritual-scientific exercises.

(8 October 1920)[63]

X asks about a child in class 3 who finds it hard to concentrate, and is unable to grasp the context in little pieces of writing.

Rudolf Steiner: Get the child to picture and recite sequences of things such as: tree: root, trunk, branch, twig, blossom, fruit. Now reverse this: fruit, blossom, twig, branch, trunk, root. Or human being: head, chest, stomach, leg, foot; foot, leg, stomach, chest, head.

(19 June 1924)[64]

Notes and references

'GA' stands for *Gesamtausgabe* or Collected Works of Rudolf Steiner in the original German. For a list of published translations see page 102.

About this book
1. GA 264, p. 135.
2. GA 16, p. 64.

1. Review of the day
3. The part of the astral or soul body transformed by the influence of the I or ego. *Manas* is a theosophical Indian term for 'spirit', and literally means 'thinking'. As the human being's fifth principle, Steiner later called it 'Spirit Self'.
4. Instructions for Adolf Arenson, in GA 267, p. 436.
5. Instructions for Amalie Wagner, in GA 264, p. 63.
6. Berlin, instructions for Camilla Wandrey, in GA 267, p. 87.
7. Berlin, instructions for Anna Wagner, in GA 264, p. 89.
8. GA 13, pp. 338 f.
9. Was ich erlebt am Tage
   Steht jetzt geistig vor mir
   So auch stelle du mein Ich
   Dich geistig vor das Bild
   Fühle wie du am Tage
   Davor gefühlt hast
   Sei mit ihm allein.
10. Lernen will ich
    Im Ich des Geistes

Zu sein wie im Leibe

Zu fühlen wie im Leibe

Zu lieben wie im Leibe

Im Lichte will ich leben

Im Lichte will ich schauen

11. Stockholm, instructions for Sophie Kinell, in GA 267, pp. 350 f.

12. Stockholm, instructions for Gustaf Kinell, in GA 267, p. 348.

13. For Mme. d'Albert, Emma Getaz, R. Lavezzari, in GA 267, pp. 232 f.

14. Astral body and astral plane: theosophical Indian terms. The astral body is also known as the body of desires or sentient body, and the astral plane as the soul world.

15. Lecture in Berlin, in GA 266/1, pp. 38–41.

16. Esoteric lesson in Stuttgart, in GA 266/1, p. 193.

17. Esoteric lesson in Stuttgart, in GA 266/1, p. 195.

18. Esoteric lesson in Berlin, in GA 266/1, pp. 199–201.

19. Esoteric lesson in Munich, in GA 266/1, p. 236.

20. Esoteric lesson in Kassel, in GA 266/1, p. 241.

21. Esoteric lesson in Dusseldorf, in GA 266/1, p. 476.

22. Esoteric lesson in Berlin, in GA 266/2, p. 447.

23. Esoteric lesson in Berlin, in GA 266/3, p. 50.

24. Lecture in Dornach, in GA 164, pp. 33–7. *Wie erlangt man Erkenntnisse der höheren Welten* [*Knowledge of the Higher Worlds*], GA 10.

2. Review of events in your life

25. Rudolf Steiner used the term 'occult' or 'esoteric' schooling in relation to the development of concealed inner capacities; and thus someone who pursued this path was described as an 'esoteric' or 'occult' pupil.

26. GA 10 [*Knowledge of the Higher Worlds*], pp. 30–2.
27. GA 15, pp. 9 f.
28. GA 16, pp. 62–4.
29. Esoteric lesson in Prague, GA 266/2, pp. 169 f.
30. Lecture in The Hague, GA 145, pp. 55–8.
31. Lecture in Munich, GA 147, pp. 141 f.

3. Review from the other's perspective
32. Lecture in Dornach, GA 179, pp. 132–4.
33. Our current cultural epoch which, according to Steiner, began around 1413 and, like the others, lasts for 2160 years.
34. The consciousness soul is the highest of the three soul aspects, and the one we need to develop in our current cultural epoch. The other, preceding soul configurations are: the sentient soul and the intellectual or mind soul. Since the consciousness soul depends on the strongest individuation, however, it can have an intrinsically antisocial quality.
35. Lecture in Dornach, GA 186, pp. 125–7.
36. Lecture in Bern, GA 186, pp. 170–4.
37. Lecture in Dornach, GA 187, p. 139.
38. Lecture in Zurich, GA 193, pp. 21 f.

4. Review exercise to comprehend karmic connections
39. Lecture in Dornach, GA 236, pp. 119–26.

5. Exercises in thinking backwards
40. This 'third thing' follows the previous two stages of knowledge of philosophy and cosmology gained through imagination and inspiration. Steiner describes these previous two stages in GA 15 (pp. 15 ff.) together with the necessary meditations.
41. GA 25, p. 19.

42. Lecture in Munich, GA 143, pp. 18 f.
43. *Kosmogonie* was published in Jena in 1916 by the Austrian philosopher and precursor of Gestalt psychology Christian von Ehrenfels (1859–1932). From 1896 to 1929, Ehrenfels was philosophy professor at the German university in Prague.
44. Lecture in Dornach, GA 170, pp. 132 f.
45. Lecture in Dornach, GA 194, pp. 199 f.
46. Lecture in Stuttgart, GA 297a, pp. 99 f.
47. Lecture in Elberfeld. This is published in a single edition entitled *Das Wesen der Anthroposophie*, Dornach 1998, pp. 32–4.
48. Lecture in Dornach, GA 210, pp. 83–5.
49. GA 10, *Knowledge of the Higher Worlds*, and GA 13, *Occult Science*.
50. Lecture in London, GA 211, pp. 156–60.
51. Lecture in Oxford, GA 214, pp. 136–8.
52. Lecture in Dornach, GA 215, pp. 35–7.
53. Lecture in Rotterdam, GA 297a, pp. 132 f.
54. This was one of the lectures that Rudolf Steiner gave to the workmen at the Goetheanum, for which they could hand in questions or themes they wished to be discussed.
55. Lecture in Dornach, GA 350, pp. 157–9.
56. Lecture in Penmaenmawr, GA 227, pp. 59–62.

6. The review and kamaloka

57. Lecture in Christiania (Oslo), GA 79, pp. 123–6.
58. Earlier in the lecture Steiner said:

    > We have to acquire the idea that the I and astral body initially do not accompany us at all in our earthly develop-ment. Basically they remain behind, remain where we are when on the verge of acquiring a physical and etheric body.

In other words, at the moment of waking up, too, our I and astral body stand at the time when our earthly life was just about to begin. Really we only pass through life on earth with our physical body and, in a strange way, with our etheric body. We only fully undergo life on earth in spatial terms and ordinary time with our physical body. Only our physical body grows old, and the etheric body connects our beginning with the point at which we stand at any particular period of our life.

(GA 226, pp. 13 f.)

59. Kamaloka is a theosophical Indian term (literally, 'the place of longing or desire') for the after-death state of soul purification. It corresponds to purgatory in Christian cosmology.
60. Lecture in Christiania (Oslo), GA 226, pp. 16–19.

7. The review and education

61. Teachers' meeting in Stuttgart, GA 300a, p. 117.
62. Teachers' meeting in Stuttgart, GA 300a, p. 124.
63. Questions and answers, Dornach, GA 297, pp. 227 f.
64. Teachers' meeting in Stuttgart, GA 300c, p. 181.

Sources

The following volumes are cited in this book. Where relevant, published editions of equivalent English translations are given below the German titles.

The works of Rudolf Steiner are listed with the volume numbers of the complete works in German, the *Gesamtausgabe* (GA), as published by Rudolf Steiner Verlag, Dornach, Switzerland.

RSP = Rudolf Steiner Press, UK
AP / SB = Anthroposophic Press / SteinerBooks, USA

GA 10   *Wie erlangt man Erkenntnisse der höheren Welten?* (1993)
         Knowledge of the Higher Words (RSP); *How to Know Higher Worlds* (SB)

GA 13   *Die Geheimwissenschaft im Umriss* (1989)
         Occult Science (RSP); *An Outline of Esoteric Science* (SB)

GA 15   *Die geistige Führung des Menschen und der Menscheit* (1987)
         Spiritual Guidance of the Individual and Humanity (AP)

GA 16   *Ein Weg zur Selbsterkenntnis des Menschen* (2004)
         A Way of Self-Knowledge (SB)

GA 25   *Drei Schritte der Anthroposophie. Philosophie—Kosmologie—Religion* (1999)

GA 79   *Die Wirklichkeit der höheren Welten* (1988)

GA 143   *Erfahrungen des Übersinnlichen. Die drei Wege der Seele zu Christus* (1994)

GA 145   *Welche Bedeutung hat die okkulte Entwicklung des*

Menschen für seine Hüllen—physischer Leib, Ätherleib, Astralleib—und sein Selbst? (1997)

Effects of Esoteric Development (SB)

GA 147   *Die Geheimnisse der Schwelle* (1997)
   Secrets of the Threshold (AP)

GA 164   *Der Wert des Denkens für eine den Menschen befriedigende Erkenntnis* (2006)

GA 170   *Das Rätsel des Menschen. Die geistigen Hintergründe der menschlichen Geschichte* (1992)
   The Riddle of Humanity (RSP)

GA 179   *Geschichtliche Notwendigkeit und Freiheit. Schicksalseinwirkungen aus der Welt der Toten* (1993)

GA 186   *Die soziale Grundforderung unserer Zeit—In geänderter Zeitlage* (1990)

GA 187   *Wie kann die Menschheit den Christus wiederfinden? Das dreifache Schattendasein unserer Zeit und das neue Christus-Licht* (1995)
   How Can Mankind Find the Christ? (AP)

GA 193   *Der innere Aspekt des sozialen Rätsels* (2007)

GA 194   *Die Sendung Michaels* (1994)

GA 210   *Alte und neue Einweihungsmethoden* (2001)
   Old and New Methods of of Initiation (RSP)

GA 211   *Das Sonnenmysterium und das Mysterium von Tod und Auferstehung* (2006)
   The Sun Mystery and The Mystery of Death and Resurrection (SB)

GA 214   *Das Geheimnis der Trinität* (1999)
   The Mystery of the Trinity (AP)

GA 215   *Die Philosophie, Kosmologie und Religion in der Anthroposophie* (1980)
   Philosophy, Cosmology and Religion (AP)

GA 226   *Menschenwesen, Menschenschicksal und Welt-Entwicklung* (1988)
Man's Being, His Destiny and World Evolution (AP)

GA 227   *Initiationserkenntnis* (2000)
The Evolution of Consciousness (RSP)

GA 236   *Esoterischer Betrachtungen karmischer Zusammenhänge. Zweiter Band* (1988)
Karmic Relationships, Vol. 2 (RSP)

GA 264   *Zur Geschichte und aus den Inhalten der ersten Abteilung der Esoterischen Schule 1904–1914* (1996)
From the History and Contents of the First Section of the Esoteric School (1904–1914) (SB)

GA 266/1   *Aus den Inhalten der esoterischen Stunden. Gedächtnisaufzeichnungen von Teilnehmern. Band I: 1904–1909* (2007)
Esoteric Lessons 1904–1914 (SB)

GA 266/2   *Aus den Inhalten der esoterischen Stunden. Gedächtnisaufzeichnungen von Teilnehmern. Band II: 1910–1912* (1996)

GA 266/3   *Aus den Inhalten der esoterischen Stunden. Gedächtnisaufzeichnungen von Teilnehmern. Band III: 1913 und 1914; 1920–1923* (1998)

GA 267   *Seelenübungen, Band I: Übungen mit Wort- und Sinnbildmeditationen zur methodischen Entwicklung höherer Erkenntniskräften, 1904–1924* (2001)

GA 297   *Idee und Praxis der Waldorfschule* (1998)
The Spirit of the Waldorf School (AP)

GA 297a   *Erziehung zum Leben* (1998)

GA 300a   *Konferenzen mit den Lehrern der Freien Waldorfschule 1919 bis 1924. Band I: 1919–1921* (1995)
Faculty Meetings with Rudolf Steiner (SB)

GA 300c   *Konferenzen mit den Lehrern der Freien Waldorfschule 1919 bis 1924. Band III: 1923–1924* (1995)
Faculty Meetings with Rudolf Steiner (SB)

GA 350   *Rhythmen im Kosmos und im Menschenwesen. Wie kommt man zum Schauen der geistigen Welt?* (1991)
From Mammoths to Mediums... (RSP)

All English-language titles are available via Rudolf Steiner Press, UK (www.rudolfsteinerpress.com) or SteinerBooks, USA (www.steinerbooks.org)

ALSO AVAILABLE:

Rudolf Steiner
Six Steps in Self-Development
The 'Supplementary Exercises'

The so-called 'supplementary exercises'—to be carried out
alongside the 'review exercises' and meditation—are integral to the
path of personal development presented by Rudolf Steiner.
Together they form a means of experiencing the spiritual realm in
full consciousness. Meditation enlivens *thinking*, the review
exercises cultivate the *will*, whilst the supplementary exercises
educate and balance *feeling*. Conscientiously practised, this path of
self-knowledge and development has the effect of opening a source
of inner strength and psychological health that soon make
themselves felt in daily life.

In six stages these exercises enable the practise of qualities that can
be summarized as: control of thoughts, initiative of will,
equanimity, positivity, open-mindedness and equilibrium of soul.
When carried out regularly, they balance possible harmful effects
of meditative practice and bring inner certainty and security to the
soul. They are also of inestimable value in their own right due to
their beneficial and wholesome effect on daily life.

In this invaluable small book, the editor has drawn together
virtually all Rudolf Steiner's statements on the supplementary
exercises, supporting them with commentary and notes. With a
chapter devoted to each exercise, they are described in detail and
from different perspectives. The final chapter contains passages
chosen to illumine specific aspects of the exercises: their sequence
and duration; their protective function; the development of the
twelve-petalled lotus flower; and the relation of the exercises to the
work of the Society founded by Rudolf Steiner.

96 pages; 978 1 85584 237 3; £9.99